1

THE
FORMULA

FOR

HAPPINESS

— AND —

SUCCESS

IN LIFE

<u>5 Key Principles to</u>

<u>Achieve Happiness and Success</u>

By Danny Cole

The Formula for Happiness and Success in Life

5 Key Principles for happiness and success

Publication date 2015

Written and published by: Danny Cole

theformulacoach.com

ISBN 978-0692421925

Library of Congress Control Number: 2015906641

Special thanks to all my family and friends who have supported me along this journey and most importantly thank you God.

Table of contents

Preface

You have just picked up the simplest self-help book ever written. Some books try to bedazzle you with big words and lengthy messages, but it is often the simplest messages that are to the point that have the greatest impact.

And, that is how this book is written. Simple to read, easy to understand, and filled with powerful life-changing information. So powerful that anyone reading it can create the life he or she desires now.

We have a culture of information overload. With all the self-help books, seminars, videos, and audio programs out there, it is easy to become overwhelmed. Where should you start? Should you grab a book, purchase an audio series, or attend a seminar? Whose books should you read? How much should you spend? Information overload rarely accomplishes anything.

Everyone wants success to start today. Not next week, next month, or next year. Everyone is looking for success and happiness, but it seems no one knows the formula for this elusive dream. This book will allow you to begin that excitement-filled journey today!

In this book, the principles of happiness and success are broken down into keys. Keys unlock doors, pathways, and vaults that protect valuables. Inside you will learn five keys. That's it. Just five simple keys. Instead of trying to read one self-help book after another, I challenge you to read this book several times. Read this book until these five keys become a part of you, unlocking all your hidden potential.

Learn just one key per day, and you will begin to see amazing changes take place in your life. Over a brief period, your life will change in ways you never imagined. This book provides a simple formula from which you can immediately apply common principles shared by all successful people. These Universal Principles will allow you to unlock the hidden power within you, just as it has for others.

As a life coach, I have taught many people what you are about to learn. And, like them, when you make the principles inside this book a part of your life, you will become one of the rare few who truly understand and live the world's most sought after dream, of happiness and success.

Why does it seem like some people have all the right friends, great relationships, and perfect finances? Why do things always seems to go their way, while other people struggle to find friends, have failed relationships, and continually face problems and hardships? Is there a reason why? And can you change the life you are living and have all the good things in life, including the right friends, fulfilling relationships and job, success, and happiness?

After years of studying those who have everything – the finest clothes, the means to vacation when and where they want, the life that keeps them smiling and simply enjoying every day to the fullest – and those who "have not," who constantly repeat defeatist clichés such as, "If I didn't have bad luck, I'd have no luck at all" and struggle to get by day to day, it hit me like a ton of bricks.

After all the research, seminars, and self-help books, all the "information overload," I finally understood the simple formula that can give you the life of your dreams. It is so simple and has been there all along, and I want to share this powerful life-changing information with you. You deserve it.

Everything you desire to have is within your grasp. Your life, your career, your relationship, everything. First, though, I want to make something clear. I'm not talking about being greedy. Greed is the opposite of what you will be learning. Greed will stop you from receiving.

Proverbs 11:24 says, "One gives freely, yet grows all the richer; another withholds what he should give, and only suffers want." Greed is negative, and we do not want negativity in our lives. I'm talking about having everything your heart desires by using this simple formula.

This formula works for everyone, regardless of religion, social standing, group affiliation, or anything else. All that matters is you have faith and believe. I am a Christian, but I will not attempt to persuade you through religion. All religions speak about faith and belief, which is an important key for unlocking the door of abundance, and the Bible is filled with verses that support these Universal Laws.

What I am telling you is that no matter what your faith, where you come from, or who you are, you can live a happy, fulfilled life if you apply the principles I describe in this book. A life overflowing with great things. A life that attracts good for you and those around you. A life that allows you to radiate a certain presence of confidence and abundance, so that everyone feels it when you enter a room.

Mark 9:23 says, "If you can believe, all things are possible to him who believes." Believe you deserve it, and it shall be given to you. This book is written for you. You can change your life this very moment, in the blink of an eye, but you must first believe.

I'll bet by now you are wanting to know the formula. These five Keys that make up The Formula for Happiness and Success in Life are simple but profound. These Keys will unlock the vault of Infinite Power and abundance that is lying inside of you.

Once you're tapped into the realm of Infinite Power and abundance within you, the possibilities are endless. You get to write the book of your life. Unlock this vault, and you unlock your dreams.

Let your journey begin…….

The Law of Attraction

"All that we are is the result of what we have thought. The mind is everything. What we think, we become."

Buddha

The Law of Attraction and its knowledge has been around since the beginning of time. But, only the privileged elite, such as rulers or royalty, were entrusted with the knowledge of its power. It was said to be kept from the masses to maintain societal control and order.

Those who were privileged to belong to the secret society of "knowledge and power" and understood the principles, believed in these principles, and applied them were able to live the lives that others only dreamed of. They did what they wanted, when they wanted.

They had more money than they knew what to do with. They attracted the perfect mate who complimented and inspired them to be even more successful. They attended social events to which others were unable to gain access. They wore the finest of clothes and traveled to vacation destinations that were inaccessible to commoners. They were chauffeured in luxurious automobiles on the way to five-star restaurants and ate the most delectable meals, while everyone else lived paycheck to paycheck, struggling just to get by.

But, now this Universal Knowledge and its power are available to you and all who read this book and are willing to apply the principles written inside.

What is the Law of Attraction? I'm glad you asked. There are a number of Universal Laws that govern our world: the Law of Cause and Effect, the Law of Action, the Law of Divine Oneness, and the Law of Gravity, to name a few.

The Law of Attraction is the belief that your thought patterns, whether positive or negative, will attract events, situations, and circumstances to you accordingly. If positive thought patterns dominate your conscious way of thinking, then you will experience positive life experiences. If, on the other hand, negative thought patterns dominate your train of thought, then, unfortunately for you, your life will be filled with negative life experiences. This is the paradigm of life.

"Decide what you want to be, do and have, think the thoughts of it, emit the frequency, and your vision will become your life"

Rhonda Byrne, The Secret

According to Jack Canfield, "The Law of Attraction states that whatever you focus and think about, read about, and talk about intensely, you're going to attract more of into your life." Your thoughts will attract to your life what you focus your attention on. Just as a magnet attracts, your focus will give power to whatever it is you focus on, and you will attract those situations, circumstances, events, and even people into your life.

Now, I want you to really think about that for a moment. Do we really attract to our lives what we think about most, good or bad? Could it be that simple? Do we really possess the power to manifest and bring into our lives what we truly desire? The answer is YES! If understood and used properly, your life, like that of rulers and royalty who know and apply the principles, can be the life others dream of having.

The principles of the Law of Attraction are written everywhere and by everyone. Napoleon Hill said, "You can be whatever you make up your mind to be. Being happy, wealthy, or successful is a product of the mind and its unlimited possibilities." William Arthur Ward said, "Nothing limits achievements like small thinking; nothing expands possibilities like unleashed thinking." James Allen said it like this, "You are today where your thoughts have brought you. You will be tomorrow where your thoughts take you."

The Bible is filled with verses that speak about the principles and power you possess, with verses such as; Matthew 21:22, "All things, whatsoever ye shall ask in prayer, believing, ye shall receive; " Matthew 7:7, "Ask and it shall be given to you; seek and you will find; knock and the door will be opened to you; "James 2:14-26, "Faith without works is dead," and, one of my favorites, Philippians 4:13, "I can do all things through Christ who strengthens me."

You just have to be ready for the enlightenment. You have to have your eyes and mind open, ready to receive the powerful Universal Knowledge that can change your life and those around you, and apply it. The power of the Law of Attraction is working on your behalf, whether you know it or not. It is working for you this very moment, whether you believe in it or not.

"Life consists of what a man is thinking about all day"

Ralph Waldo Emerson

Would you like an example of the Law of Attraction at work? Have you ever talked about, or even thought about, a friend you have not heard from in a while, and then, out of the blue that person called you or you ran into him or her while you were out running errands? Or have you ever had an unexpected expense come up and you weren't sure how you could pay for it, and then, out of nowhere, somehow the money came to you?

When I was twenty-two years old I was the manager for a game room furniture store that was about an hour from my home. It was a fun job. We sold billiard tables, poker tables, pinball machines, etc. and I got to play with them all on a daily basis. You couldn't ask for a better job at twenty-two.

Twenty minutes into my drive home from work one evening, I had a flat tire. When I took the car to the tire shop the following day to purchase a new tire, I was quickly informed by one of the employees that I needed not just one tire, but a new set of four tires.

I had been driving on the same set of tires since I had purchased the car, and all four tires were worn to the point that the steel belts were showing. Without a doubt, I needed an entire new set.

When the employee told me this, I had just $40.00 in my checking account. I had no idea how I was going to purchase the set of tires I desperately needed.   Yet, currently being aware of the power of thought I learned from my recent reading of *"The Power of your Subconscious Mind"* by Dr. Joseph Murphy, I said to myself, "I have the money for my brand new set of tires, now."

When I returned home that afternoon, waiting for me in the mailbox was a check from my mortgage company. Due to an error, I had been overcharged on my property taxes and had been sent a check for just over $600.00. Can you guess how much the new set of tires cost? Just a few dollars shy of the amount I received from the mortgage company. This is the Law of Attraction at work.

What about children at Christmas time? They have no idea about the Law of Attraction or what it does. All they know is that they ask Santa Claus for toys and other items they want for Christmas. Children do this with the full expectation, excitement, and belief that they will be waking up on Christmas Day with a burst of energy to run downstairs, wide-eyed and ready to open and enjoy everything Santa brought them.

They do not doubt. They ask, they believe they will receive, and they receive most, if not all, of what they asked for. Now, children do not have jobs that will pay money to purchase these presents they want, do they? They are pure and innocent and are not weighed down with self-perceived limitations. Are you starting to get the "Aha!" moment now? This is just a small example of the Law of Attraction at work.

I'm sure right now you can think of some experiences in your life during which this Universal Law was at work for you. What are they? Was it running into a friend you were talking about recently? Was it getting the perfect parking spot while at the mall? Was it receiving a job offer you wanted? Or, maybe the person you were admiring asked you out? What was your experience?

I have a friend who owns a walk-in medical clinic in Newnan, Georgia. I was at his office one Saturday morning getting a routine blood pressure check-up, and as we were chatting the topic of the Law of Attraction came up. He was unfamiliar with it. "Is it like ESP or déjà vu, or something along those lines?" he asked.

I explained to him just what you finished reading and some of what you will be reading later in this chapter. It is as simple as, "You think it, you will bring it." You just have to have your eyes open and be aware. Before I left he and I planned to meet for lunch the following Monday.

While looking over the menu he began to tell me about something that had happened on the Sunday after we had last seen each other. He said he was thinking about the discussion we had and began to recall times in his life where the Law of Attraction could have occurred.

He described how, on the way to church, he asked his teenage daughter if she knew anything about the Law of Attraction and, if so, what she thought about it. She replied that she was very aware of it and believed in it. This intrigued him even more.

He then proceeded to tell me that he had his daughter look up certain verses in Exodus and read them aloud so they could discuss them. This is something he practices on a regular basis so they can learn and grow in the Word together. He looked at me after telling me this and said, "Danny, guess what the sermon was about on Sunday?"

Before I could say anything, with excitement and enthusiasm in his voice, he answered, "The exact verses my daughter and I were discussing right after talking about the Law of Attraction! I couldn't believe it. It was amazing. We were talking about it, and then, THERE IT WAS!"

The Law of Attraction, along with the other four keys, discussed in later chapters of this book, will require a shift in the paradigm of your conscious thinking. Once the shift takes place, your life will never be the same. You will be aware of the events going on in your life and began to see that you are at the cause of, instead of at the effect of, these events.

Once this happens, your confidence will grow like a small ball of snow rolling down a snow-covered mountain. At the beginning of its journey down the mountain, it is small and easy to stop. But once it gets going and grabs momentum and continues down the mountain, it grows larger and larger and, eventually, turns into an avalanche of unstoppable force, and nothing in its path can stop it! YOU, LIKE THE AVALANCHE, WILL BE UNSTOPPABLE!

"Thoughts are magnetic, and thoughts have a frequency. As you think thoughts, they are sent out into the Universe, and they magnetically attract all like things that are on the same frequency"

Rhonda Byrne, The Secret

Energy and the Law of Attraction

Through quantum physics, we have learned that we are all "pure energy." Everyone and everything is pure energy and vibrates at a certain frequency. Have you ever shuffled your feet across the carpet and then touched someone? What happened? If you are like most people, the person you touched received a small electrical shock that resulted from the transfer of energy.

Scientists, with the technology we currently have, are able to look deep within a person. Beneath the protective layer of skin. Beneath the dense bone that helps the body to stay rigid. Even beneath the atom which was once thought to be the smallest element of humans. They have discovered that the atom is made up of subatomic particles, and these particles are pure energy. That's right. You are pure energy.

The Universe and everything contained within it is pure energy. Everything from you, me, the chair in which you are sitting, to the sun and the stars in the sky, are all energy. Energy, like God, can be neither created nor destroyed. From a spiritual aspect, we all come from God.

At the very essence of your soul, is this extreme force of energy that is at work on your behalf every second of every day. You may call it Infinite Power, Infinite Mind, God, the Universe, or another name, but rest assured this powerful, never-ceasing creative energy is flowing through you to manifest your internal thoughts to external reality.

This energy vibrates at a certain frequency, depending upon what is focused on and your emotional state at the time and it is being sent out into the Universe and will return to you what it resonates with.

Have you stopped and thought about why certain groups of people associate with others like themselves? You see these diverse groups of people on a daily basis: for instance, those who are athletic, or those who always have drama going on in their lives. What about the wealthy, or those living in poverty, or those who are always happy and having fun?

Why do they associate with others like themselves? Do you think it is just by coincidence? Or, do you think they could have been drawn to one another by their habitual thought patterns?

I'm sure, right now, you can think of that friend who always has something to complain about. Every time you talk to that person, he or she always has something negative to report, and there is no shyness or holding back, is there?

If you are like me, when you see that name appear on the phone you sigh a little sigh because you already know this conversation is going to tax your energy level. Such people always have a new "did you hear about so and so" or "you are not going to believe this" story of negative, energy-draining gossip to share.

Or, they will complain about how horrible the economy is or their lack of money to make ends meet, or they might tell you that a friend's relationship is in turmoil. Or, how about those friends who are always complaining about how sick they always are, or how, if they didn't have bad luck, they would have no luck at all?

There is truth in the old saying "misery loves company," but in reality, it is more like "misery attracts the same company." The energy that miserable people put out will attract the same miserable energy in return.

The type of people who are always complaining also carry the same circle of friends, so be sure you are not in that circle, or else you could be attracting more negative stories to contribute to the gossip circle.

You must remember your thoughts and words have power. If you speak it you will bring it, good or bad. The author of *The Secret*, Rhonda Byrne explains the connection with our thoughts and what it attracts clearly in this statement - "Thoughts are magnetic, and thoughts have a frequency. As you think thoughts, they are sent out into the Universe, and they magnetically attract all like things that are on the same frequency."

Now I want you to think of another type of person, but this time someone who is wealthy. Think about someone who just seems to have their finances and their career in an extraordinary state of success.

What does that person think about? What does he or she talk about? I can guarantee you that it is not about a lack of money. The topics of discussion such people are involved in on a regular basis are centered around investing, real estate, stocks and bonds, and money markets, to name a few. These people discuss topics that will propel them towards their financial goals and desires.

Now, who does this type of person associate with? He or she will associate with or "attract" others who vibrate at the same frequency. They will attract those who are members of the same exclusive clubs and those who take exotic vacations all over the world at the spur of the moment.

The person who is wealthy will also attract those who live in large homes with all the amenities, from a theater room, a bar, a game room, a pool in the backyard surrounded by a beautiful green lawn carefully manicured and landscaped, just like them. They will also find themselves attending the same fundraiser events together.

What about people you know who are athletic? What do they do? Do they sit around watching television all day long or are they actively involved in physical activities such as running and biking?

Do you see them frequenting fast-food restaurants and stuffing their faces with mind-numbing calories or taking care of their bodies by taking in the right types of healthy, balanced meals?

What do they enjoy talking about? Would it be a favorite television show or a new workout routine they are excited to try?

The common denominator among this affiliation of friends will be achieving personal physical fitness goals, i.e., those who are improving their athletic abilities or, at the very least, those who are maintaining a healthy lifestyle that will enable them to look and feel better.

So, the question is why are certain types of people attracted to and associate with one another? Is it because they are told to? No. They are attracted to one another because of the way they think. They have the same thought patterns. Those thought patterns put off certain vibrations (vibes) that attracts those same vibes in return. They resonate with one another.

I'm sure you have heard someone say, "I really like that person. We're on the same page." Well, what that person is saying is that they resonate at the same frequency as the other person. The vibrational frequency that is being sent out is attracting similar people, events, and situations that resonate at the same frequency. This is the reason people are drawn to one another. This is the reason certain people seem to just "click" or "hit it off."

"The predominant thought or mental attitude is the magnet, and the law is that like attracts like"

Charles Haanel

A simple way to think of it is like this. You are a walking, talking magnet. As a walking, talking magnet, you are endowed with special abilities. The strongest ability you possess is an extraordinarily strong magnetic field. This magnetic field will attract to you or repel from you circumstances, situations, and even people, depending upon whether you are magnetized to them or not.

You are magnetized to the situations, circumstances, and people by the thoughts you put out into the Universe, and, in turn, you repel those that do not resonate with you. Your feelings and beliefs behind the thoughts you create are what determine how powerful your thoughts are. They also determine how quickly they will come back to you.

Your thoughts are like a boomerang, and the more belief and feelings the thoughts possess the quicker they are sent out and the quicker they will come back to you.

Once you become aware of how your reality is formed, through your thoughts and beliefs, then you will be able to begin a new journey in life. A journey that will enable you to create and control the reality you desire.

What we think affects our emotions. Our emotions in turn affect our actions, which in turn determine the results we gain in any given situation. The power of the Universal Law of Attraction first begins in your mind. The thoughts you think, the feelings you experience, and the ideas you create, are held in your infinite mind. This is where it starts.

The more emotions you combine with the thought the more powerful the thought becomes. The more powerful the thought becomes the quicker it can manifest in your life.

Your perceptions are always creating your reality. It creates it from the energy of your thoughts. The Infinite Mind of

God is within you and supplies your thoughts with the energy to create.

Whatever your thoughts are focused on, you are supplying energy for the vision behind those thoughts to be created. The more energy we give a thought the more power it has and the sooner it can manifest.

"All things are you ask for in prayer, believing, you will receive"

Matthew 21:22

ASK, BELIEVE, AND RECEIVE

Now that we have discussed the power of your thoughts and how they are able to create your reality, let's talk a little about choices, belief, and the simple process of *Ask, Believe, and Receive*. The simple process of Ask, Believe, and Receive can allow the Law of Attraction to work for you quickly and easily.

Choice and belief are everything. The way you choose to think right now is just that, a choice. Think about it, EVERYTHING is a choice. You make choices all day long, every day of your life. You choose whether you get out of bed or sleep in a little longer.

You choose whether you are going to dress up or dress down for the day. You choose what you want for breakfast or whether you will even eat breakfast. You choose whether you will go to work or not.

These are but a few choices you make in the very beginning of your day. It's that simple. Your life is a series of choices, and you have to make a choice about how you want to live it. Your level of success is equal to your level of commitment to the choices you make.

No one is forcing you to do anything. Everything is a choice. Once you become consciously aware of this fact and understand that everything is a choice then you can begin to make the choices that will benefit you and your life. You can begin to make the choices that will put you and your destiny of abundance in alignment.

What you choose and what you believe will dictate what you attract. The great thing about choices and beliefs is that you are in total control of them both. You get to choose what you think and what you believe. A belief is just an idea that has been reinforced by experiences. A belief can be true or false. It doesn't matter.

Some people believe that money is evil, while others believe that money is great. The reason one person believes one thing while another person believes the total opposite is based on either the experiences an individual has had with money or the things they have been told by others about it. Money, in reality, is just a piece of paper.

How to change a belief

First. Doubt the old belief. By questioning a belief, it cracks the foundation and opens up the opportunity to disprove it and remove it, so that a new belief can take its place. A belief YOU want to have instead of a belief that was programmed there by either the media or someone else's opinions and ideas.

Second. You want to state the new idea (beliefs first begin as ideas) and recall experiences that will reinforce that idea. Just as the old belief was reinforced by someone saying, for example, "money is the root of all evil" or "to be wealthy, you have to take advantage of others," you can now begin to reinforce the new belief by recalling experiences that convey the idea that money is good.

For example, you can begin to say things such as "I need to have money in order to donate to worthy causes," or "Money allows me to help people in their time of need," and "With money, I can provide my family with life's necessities as well as enjoying a tropical vacation."

Reinforce the new idea with as many "things" as possible. Think of it as giving legs to a table. The more legs the table has, the sturdier it will be. If the table only has one or two legs, it will most likely not stand. But, give the table fifty legs and see how strong it becomes.

Third. After you doubt the old belief and state the new idea and reinforce it, you will need to take the third and final step, which is conditioning the idea. Just like working out to reach peak physical condition. You can't work out just one time and think you will be in the best shape of your life. You need to condition yourself by working out on a consistent basis. The same goes for an idea that you want to transform into a belief. After a period of time, the idea will be reinforced enough so that it becomes a BELIEF.

By making the right choices, you will bring true happiness and success to all areas of your life. Once you change your internal habitual thought pattern, you can change your external world. Everything is a choice, so make sure you are making the right ones. Your choices will determine your destiny.

"It is in your moments of decision that your destiny is shaped"

Anthony Robbins

Your destiny is determined by the choices you make, good or bad, and now you get to consciously make those choices. Look at it like this: It is as if you have a catalog right in front you, and this catalog is titled "CHOICES." It is laid out very simple, once you open it up. On the left side of the page is a single list of positive words: one positive word beneath the other, from the top of the page to the bottom. On the right side of the page, directly across, is a list of words that are polar opposites.

Now, here is the fun and empowering part. You get to go down each page and choose what YOU want! Not what anyone else wants for you. You get to choose what you want from each set of words.

Choose to be happy. Choose to be successful. Choose to be full of energy. Choose to be the best person you can be. Choose to read this life- changing book. Choose to be in the best relationship. Choose to be wealthy. Choose to be more intuitive. Choose to be a better parent. Choose to be a better boss. Choose what YOU want.

You can choose to believe what you want to believe. You can choose to believe in yourself. It is that simple. Your life is a choice, and you have to make a choice on how you want to live IT. I would suggest you make choices that are self-empowering, choices that will set you free from self-imposed limitation, choices that allow you to be free, happy, and successful. Choose to be BLESSED!

"You don't have to see the whole stair case, just take the first step"

Dr. Martin Luther King, Jr.

The Ask, Believe, and Receive process

Now that we have discussed the power of your thoughts and how they are able to create your reality and we have discussed everything being a choice, let's talk a little about the simple process that will allow the Law of Attraction to work quickly and easily for you. The process of; Ask, Believe, and Receive.

ASK. The first step in the simple process of *Asking, Believing, and Receiving* is asking. Ask or make a conscious decision about what it is you truly want for your life. You need to be crystal clear about what it is you want, with as much detail as possible. The Universe takes your thoughts and words very literally and will give you what you ask for.

You must also have clear intentions on what it is you want. You can't want one thing one day and then the very next day, want something different. You can't say, "Today I want to be with John, we have the perfect relationship in which we uplift, motivate, and nurture one another," and then, the very next day, because the two of you got into an argument, say, "I want to be with John's best friend, Nick, because John is a jerk."

This sends mixed signals into your subconscious mind and out into the Universe and can delay anything from manifesting. You must state what you want with clear intentions, with as much detail as possible, and visualize it. Clear pictures will equal clear manifestations.

Jim was telling me how he hadn't had a vacation in over 7 years. Jim currently has a successful landscaping and lawn care business but was a very successful real-estate investor just years earlier. Unfortunately, however, when the economy crashed and the real-estate bubble burst, Jim lost everything.

He had all of his money tied up in properties and had to file bankruptcy. He had no savings or assets. He was left with only his home and the possessions inside. Because of his dismal financial situation, Jim often found himself having to skip meals and when he did eat most of his meals were ordered from the dollar menus at various fast-food restaurants.

Jim, like so many others, had to start all over when the economy crashed. He vowed to himself that he would never be stuck in a financial state like that again. He said he never wanted to worry about how the bills were going to be paid or where the next meal would come from.

The only work Jim could find, after the loss of his real estate business, was cutting grass at a local lawn-care company. Through hard work and by saving everything he earned, he eventually had enough money to purchase the small business.

He was now the owner of the small lawn-care company rather than just an employee. Remembering his vow to himself, Jim poured all of his time and energy into growing his new company into one of the most successful lawn-care businesses in town.

The income from the business met all his financial needs, and allowed him to save more than enough money, pay off his home, and even make a few real-estate investments. And yet, he focused all his time on making money and never took a vacation to enjoy the fruits of his labor.

When Jim told me he was taking a week off to relax and take a vacation, I immediately asked where he was going. I was curious to see where a man who hadn't taken a vacation in 7 years would go.

I was sure it would be a resort somewhere exotic and relaxing. I envisioned beautiful beaches with staff waiting on him hand and foot. He nonchalantly told me he wasn't sure yet, but he was excited and couldn't wait for the much-needed vacation.

The next time I saw Jim was about 3 weeks later. With excitement and curiosity, I asked Jim where he had gone for vacation. His response was one I was not expecting, but I clearly understood. He said he didn't go anywhere. He wasn't sure where he wanted to go, so he just stayed home, ran errands, and took care of things around the house.

"Successful people ask better questions, and as a result, they get better answers"

Anthony Robbins

Don't miss out on the unlimited possibilities the Universe is waiting to pour out over you and your life by not knowing what it is you want. If you do not know what you want, or, in Jim's case, do not know where you want to go, then anything will do. This is why it is imperative that you know with clear detail and intention what it is you want.

Be mindful of how you ask the God or the Universe for what you desire. Once you know the questions to ask, you want to state those questions as affirmative declarations. You can't just say, "I want more money" and expect to become a millionaire, because if someone gives you a dollar, then guess what? You just received what you were asking for, more money.

I had a friend tell me he was going to win the lottery. Playing the lottery is something he and most Americans take part in each week, either with scratch-offs or drawings held on certain nights of the week.

My friend purchased the lottery ticket and said with conviction, "I'm going to win the lottery tonight!" Guess what? He did! He won the lottery that night, for $2.00. He asked for what he wanted, believed it and received it. He just failed to be detailed in his request.

Make sure you do not form your affirmative declarations as if you are expecting results in the future. Avoid saying things like "I will be rich and successful," or "I am going to have a great relationship," or "I will lose 20 pounds. These affirmations will keep your desires just out of reach.

You will almost have them, but something will always seem to come up and block them from you. These types of statements are telling the Universe what you want, but that you don't want it now; you want it later.

You want to state and confirm your wants, your desires, in the present. After all we are not promised tomorrow. The only time we truly live is now.

We can't live in the past, because it has already happened. We can't live in the future, because it is not here yet, and when it does arrive, it will be the now. So, the only time we truly have is now, so you want to state your affirmations in the present, as if you already have them. Stating your desires in the present is key.

If my friend had affirmed, "I won the lottery for $4 million dollars" on the specific date, then who knows? Maybe he would have had a different outcome.

You have to state your questions as positive affirmations. An affirmation is a word or group of words that transcends our realm of thinking in the present and is sent out into the Universe to create our future.

These affirmations are planted into our subconscious mind and are sent out into the Universe, where Infinite Power can grow them and shape them into our reality.

If it is the car of your dreams you want, one way to ask for it could be, "I have the car of my dreams. It is a beautiful

Grigio Silverstone Ferrari 458 Spider with charcoal interior. I love to drive it everywhere."

Imagine the feeling you get while starting up the engine and hearing it run. Feel the power at your fingertips as you press the gas pedal and begin to accelerate. Feel the wind in your hair and the slightly envious looks you receive as you drive down the street. Feel it in your heart.

You are a child of God, The Universe, The Giver, and He wants to bless you. If your desire or "want" is for a raise at work, then ask for it. If it is for a better relationship than your last one or the one you are currently in, then ask for it. If it is for that new car you have had your eye on, then ask for that too! You have to know what it is you want. Be specific and detailed, and ask for it.

BELIEVE. So, making a conscious decision on what you want for your life, or *ASKING*, is the first step toward achieving it. After choosing what you want, the next and most crucial element of this simple process is *BELIEF*. The Merriam-Webster dictionary defines belief as "a feeling of being sure that someone or something exists or that something is true."

You must, without a shadow of a doubt, believe in your choice. Believe you are going to receive it like children at Christmas believe they will receive the toys they want. You too must desire and believe you will receive what you want.

You must believe you will receive "it" no matter what "it" is. You have to strip yourself from the self-imposed limitations: self-imposed limitations on your finances, on your health, on your relationship, on your capability of learning, on anything that is holding you back from living the life of your dreams. Break the chains of disbelief and set yourself free.

You have to desire what it is you are asking for. Without strong internal desire, there will be no external manifestation. Desire is what gives your vibrational frequency the strength and power to return back to you. What you desire most will manifest.

What this means is that you will need to feel as though you have already received what it is you were asking for. In order to see change, you must see things as you hope them to be, not as they are. You must fully and truly believe that what you think internally will become external reality.

For instance, if you desire to drop a few pounds and get into great physical condition, but you have a stronger desire to go home after work and be lazy, then guess what? Your desire to be lazy is more pleasurable and, therefore, is stronger than your desire to get into great shape, so you will go home after your day and be lazy. The stronger desire will win every time.

You want your desire to be as strong as possible. Desire is the fuel for your success. In order to know how strong your desire is, you will need to ask yourself a few simple questions.

Discover your Desire Power

In order to do this little exercise, you will first need to grab a piece of paper and something to write with. Title the paper "My Desires." Next, write down these questions and answer them.

The answer might only be one sentence or it could be an entire paragraph, it doesn't matter. Keep in mind there are no wrong answers here, so just be honest and truthful with yourself.

What does my desire mean to me?

How important is my desire?

Will my desire help improve my life?

In what areas will my desire improve my life?

Will my desire help those around me?

Is my desire a need, or just a want?

Will my desire make me happy?

Will my desire make me a better person?

What will happen if I do not receive my desire?

This does two things for you. It reinforces, with firm motives and emotions, why you want your desire and sends it out into the Universe, allowing you to become consciously aware of the pain it will cause if you do not receive it.

You want your desire to be a NEED. A want is simply a daydream. A want is something that sounds nice, but you do not have to have it. So the desire has to be a need. Period. You must NEED what is internally desired.

If you are swimming underwater and get caught on something that is causing you to be trapped and unable to reach the surface for air, at first you will only want to get free. There is no panic, yet. You still have plenty of air in your lungs.

But, soon the air that once filled your lungs will be used, and that "want" to reach the surface will quickly turn into a need. As soon as you feel the air being depleted, panic will set in. You will then need to get free. If you do not get free, you will not reach the surface for air, and you will not live to see another day.

A need will put your manifestation power into overdrive. A need will cause you to manifest your destiny and truly live.

You must actually believe you are the owner of a successful business that allows you to make a small fortune while at the same time helping others. You must believe you are in the perfect relationship that most people only fantasize about having. You must believe in your heart of hearts that you are happy, funny, and charismatic, if those are the characteristic traits you wish to possess.

RECEIVE. The last part and, coincidentally, the part everyone likes the most, *receiving*. In order to receive, you must feel as though you have already received. If it is winning you want, then you need to feel as though you have already won. Think about it. How would a winner act? How would a winner feel? How would a winner walk and talk? Be the winner.

If what you want is to be in great physical condition and shape, then think about how the clothes will fit. Think about the looks you will receive when you are out in public. Imagine the feeling you will have when you receive the compliments. Think about how you will eat and train to maintain this physical condition.

Sometimes you have to get out of your own way to receive. Do not block what you deserve to have. Do not allow yourself to be the reason you do not have the life you want.

Expect to receive money, love, compliments, good times, surprises, assistance, free opportunities, vacations, raises, increased intelligence, increased self-esteem, empowerment, success, happiness, and everything else you want in life.

Once you begin to receive what you desire, life will become more interesting. You will begin to manifest more and more, and on a grander scale. God does not have limits. We are the ones who put self-imposed limitations on things in our lives. Nothing is too small or too big for Him to create. Keep in mind that He created the heavens and the earth. So, I'm pretty sure he can create your desires, too.

When you first begin to consciously use the Law of Attraction to attract your heart's desires, you will need to practice on a daily basis. You will need to visualize your desire every day for several minutes at a time.

Find a quiet place: somewhere with no distractions and no interruptions by cell phones, television, or people. You want a place where you can be free from all disturbances and worry so you can just be still and relax your mind. Mediation is one of the best ways to reach the mental state that will enable you to manifest with ease.

You have been given free will to do as you please. At this very moment, you could choose to put this book down and stop learning, or you can continue to read, enhance your knowledge, and learn and believe in the principles that can change your life forever.

You could even scream at the top of your lungs right now, although others around you might look at you a little funny, or you could choose to sit up straight, smile, and feel confident and relaxed. Again, it's your choice. You just have to decide to make a decision and go with it. Again, your level of success will depend on your level of commitment.

The Law of Attraction and the Infinite Power running through your body right now, is working on your behalf to create the life you desire. Like a magnet, the Law of

Attraction is drawing to you circumstances, situations, and people from the frequencies you are sending out into the Universe.

By thinking positively, you will resonate with and manifest into your reality the positive experiences life has to offer, but if you think negatively, then you will manifest negative experiences.

Most people over complicate things. They believe that if it is not a long drawn out complicated equation then it can't be right. I challenge you to not over complicate things. Keep it simple. Ask, Believe, and Receive.

Some may say they have tried to use the Law of Attraction but it doesn't work. Well, with that attitude, it will not. You must believe it's going to work. The secret is getting all of your emotions involved and BELIEVING. If you do not believe, then you will not manifest. Remember, what you truly believe in your heart of hearts will be true.

Ralph Waldo Emerson said, "The most valuable talent you can develop is that of developing your thoughts towards that of what you want." If you remember one thing remember that your thoughts create your world.

Whatever you focus on you will think about and whatever you think about, with emotion, you will bring about. Focus is everything. Anthony Robbins said, "Whatever you focus on you will be great at."

Notes

Understanding the Law of Attraction is the first Key to unlocking the door to happiness and success in your life.

FORGIVENESS

"The weak cannot forgive. Forgiveness is an attribute of the strong"

Gandhi

Right now, all over this country, and in fact, all over the world, there are people who are suffering. People just like you and me. These people come from all walks of life. They come from different backgrounds, ethnic groups, and social statuses. They speak different languages, have different physical attributes, and different personalities. Some come from single-parent households, while others come from households where both parents are together. Yet they all have one thing in common: they are suffering.

I'm not talking about suffering from hunger, even though some face that hardship, and I'm not talking about suffering from a disability, even though that is common as well. What they are suffering from is the demolisher of internal happiness called unforgiveness.

For a number of people, forgiveness will be the toughest key to possess. This key will require a shift in the paradigm of who possesses the power when one forgives. This will require you to release, rather than rehearse, past hurts. Once you possess this key, you can achieve true freedom.

Unforgiveness

If you can, I want you to think about it like this; having unforgiveness in your heart is like being a kid and wanting to play on the ultimate playground, and we will call this ultimate playground "Happy Land." Happy Land has every toy and ride imaginable.

You see other kids sliding down huge twisting slides of red, blue, and yellow, being deposited into a large foam pits. Some are jumping on trampolines, doing flips. Others are on the swings, swinging so high it looks as though they are touching the sky. Everyone there is laughing and having the time of their life.

Just looking at it causes your eyes to grow wider and brighter as an ear-to-ear smile spreads uncontrollably across your face. You see the other kids having fun, and every ounce of your body wants to be on the other side of the fence with all the other kids, partaking in all the fun.

There is just one problem.

There is only one gate that allows entry into this dreamland of carefree fun, and it is guarded by the biggest bully you have ever seen. He seems to be 10 feet tall and as wide as the gate that separates you from Happy Land.

He stands there with his beady little predator eyes, staring intently with arms crossed, towering over everyone who approaches. Questioning anyone who wants to enter into

Happy Land. He asks each kid who steps up to the gate a simple single question, "Who are you mad at?"

If you are mad at someone, you have unresolved anger and resentment. Anger plus resentment equal unforgiveness. If there is unforgiveness in your heart, you will not gain entry into Happy Land – not until you truly forgive and let go.

Letting go sounds so simple. And if you have ever let go, then you know there is something wonderful and liberating in doing so.

Letting go of the past. Letting go of hurt. Letting go of mistakes. Letting go of limitations. Letting go of unhealthy relationships. Letting go of unforgiveness. Letting go of anything that is holding you back from being free and from living the life you deserve. Letting go of negativity grants you power. Holding on only gives you a false sense of power.

"Forgiveness – This needs to be the greatest skill."

Anthony Robbins

Forgiveness is a funny thing. The view on who has the power when forgiveness takes place is all too often distorted. T.D. Jakes has said, "We think that forgiveness is weakness, but it's absolutely not; it takes a very strong person to forgive."

It would seem that the forgiver holds the position of power because the forgiver is the one who can either grant forgiveness or withhold it. However, in reality, true power is gained by forgiving.

Holding on to thoughts that produce negative emotions, such as mistakes you have made, betrayals by someone you trusted, or an unhealthy relationship with a significant other or friend, will only cause a person NOT to heal and NOT to grow. Holding onto negativity will poison you emotionally.

Buddha once said, "Holding on to bitterness and unforgiveness is like drinking poison and expecting the other person to die." The one who consumes the poison is the one who will be poisoned – no one else. So why do so many of us get caught up in drinking the poison of unforgiveness?

I'm glad you asked. Because forgiveness can be a tough, pride-filled pill to swallow, and we just do not want to force that big pill down our throats. It can also be a pill that takes off the blinders to reality and grant self-awareness, and some people just do not want that.

Some people have found their identity in all the hurt, and – whether they know it or not – do not want to let it go. They feel it gives them a reason to act the way they do, or a reason they failed at something in life, or a reason they cannot achieve and excel in life.

To them, it simply it gives them an "out card" on life. They tend to say things like, "The reason I scream and argue when I get frustrated is because that's how my parents always handled disagreements." Or, "The reason this relationship is failing is because I was cheated on in the past, so now I don't trust the person I'm with." Or, "The reason I can't do better in life is because I don't have anyone to encourage me to do better."

Failing to take responsibility for your life by making excuses and refusing to grant forgiveness when it should be granted is only an irresponsible, weak, and passive way to live life. If you are passive in life then life will be passive with you. Unforgiveness is disempowering and only robs you of the power and happiness you deserve.

I want you to remember this important distinction. This is very important. Forgiveness does not equal condoning. Forgiveness simply says, "I will not let the past control my future." If you are holding on to the past, you cannot receive the blessings God wants to give you.

To prove this to you, I want you to imagine something for a moment. Imagine your life and everything in it, is going perfectly. You are in a relationship with your true love and you couldn't be happier. Despite the troubled relationships you've had in the past, you still have opened yourself up emotionally and offered this person everything you have, completely and wholeheartedly. Every ounce of love and trust.

You have never been unfaithful or have even entertained the thought of another person. Then, out of nowhere, this person confesses to cheating on you. And now, he or she asks for your forgiveness.

Could you forgive this person? Think about it. The person you loved with every fiber of your being just told you he or she stepped outside of your sacred boundaries. Could you grant forgiveness, or would you hold on to that forgiveness?

What would happen if you didn't forgive? Would the other person suffer, or would you suffer? The answer is that both of you would suffer, but YOU would suffer more. Why would you suffer more? I'm glad you asked.

I want you to imagine your left arm is extended, palm facing up, and it is holding on to bitterness and resentment, and your right arm is extended equally as far, palm facing upward as well, and in its clutches is unforgiveness. At this moment, you're holding on tightly. Squeezing with all your might.

You feel justified for feeling the way you do. After all, why should you grant forgiveness to someone who does not deserve it? Why should you let that person be free after what he or she has done to you? You weren't in the wrong. You were innocent in all of this.

But, in the midst of your justifying to yourself why you can and should hold on and not let go, God comes along with all of His love and infinite abundance and says, "Here, I want to give you inner peace and the best relationship you could imagine." So now you need to reach out and grab this blessing God wants to give you.

But wait! Hold on. Remember, you are still holding on to bitterness, resentment, and unforgiveness, so right now both of your hands are full. You can't grab anything else. In order for you to receive the blessings that are waiting for you, you must first let go of what you are holding onto so tightly. If you do not let go, you will not be able to receive. So, in reality, the one who loses is you.

By not forgiving, you are the one who is consumed with the inner turmoil that results from repeatedly replaying the situation or conversation in your head. No one else.

You are the one thinking about it when you wake in the morning or while you are in the shower. You are the one thinking about it on the way to work or school, or at the gym, or zoning out of a conversation you are supposed to be engaged in, or when you lay your head down at night to get some rest after a long day. You see, you are the one suffering, not the person you refuse to forgive.

In fact, the person who committed this transgression might not even be aware that he or she hurt you. This person's days and nights are not filled with the same thoughts that are consuming you. To be honest, they might not even care that it happened.

Or, they may indeed be suffering, lashing out at others to make themselves feel better or, at the very least, to make someone else's day as bad as their own. Or, another scenario – and I know I have been guilty of this from time to time – is to catch only part of a conversation and take it the wrong way, subsequently creating an elaborate false representation of what was really said, only to get my own little feelings hurt.

Has that ever happened to you? Either way, whether it was intentional, unintentional, or because you may have misinterpreted what was said or done, the point here is that you are the one suffering, not the other person. You have to let go and move forward in the right direction.

You cannot move forward if you are constantly looking back. Think about it. How can you be happy if you choose to constantly think angry and resentful thoughts?

You can never be free of bitterness if you continue to think about how hurt you are from the actions of someone else. Thoughts of bitterness cannot create joy, no matter how justified you feel. No matter what the other person did to you, if you do not let go of the past, you will never be free. Forgiving yourself and others, will release you from your past.

"It's one of the greatest gifts you can give yourself, to forgive. Forgive everybody."

Maya Angelou

Forgiving yourself is vital to your ability to live a healthy and prosperous life. If you do not forgive yourself, then you are going to damage your self-esteem and block the blessings coming to you. (The next chapter addresses self-esteem in detail)

According to Dr. Michael Barry, director of pastoral care at the Cancer Treatment Centers of America, "There is a direct correlation between unforgiveness and our immune system, which directly affects our healing processes."

Moreover, according to an article by David B. Feldman, Ph.D., in psychologytoday.com, researchers for the National Comorbidity Survey asked the question, "Would you say this is true or false? I've held grudges against people for years." Of the 10,000 people surveyed just over 6,500 responded.

It was reported that those who held grudges had significantly more health problems than those who didn't. The "grudge holders" tended to have an array of health issues ranging from elevated blood pressure, to headaches, to back problems, to higher rates of heart disease compared with those who did not hold grudges and forgave.

Sometimes we need to forgive ourselves for continuing to stay in a relationship we know is unhealthy. We need to forgive ourselves for allowing people to pick on us and put us down. Sometimes we may see someone else getting picked on, yet we fail to do anything about it, and we in turn feel guilty.

We may feel we should have stepped in and done something to stop someone from going through what we have been through, but the fear of it happening to us again is overwhelming, and we turned a blind eye to the situation.

Sometimes we need to forgive ourselves for spreading rumors and talking behind other people's backs. You may need to forgive yourself for not being there in someone's time of need. Or maybe you lied to someone or broke someone's heart by cheating on them. Whatever it is, forgive yourself and let it go. Free yourself from bondage. You hold the power to set yourself free.

Sometimes, a situation that needs forgiveness may have been completely out of your control, yet you still blame yourself or others involved.

My dad died at the very young age of 42. One afternoon while at the house, he was walking to the pantry with my younger brother in tow, and suddenly, out of nowhere, he had a heart attack. At the time, my brother was just 12 years old, and sadly, he watched our father fall to the floor while grabbing his chest in agony.

Panic-stricken, my brother ran through the house to find help. By the time my little brother reached the rest of our family, his little face had already lost all color due to sheer panic and the fright of witnessing what had just happened to our dad. He got everyone's attention and had them follow him to where our dad lay motionless on the floor.

My brother called 911 as my sister began administering chest compressions and my mom performed mouth-to-mouth resuscitation until the paramedics arrived. Even with everyone doing what they could, my dad still passed away, right there in front of everyone.

I still vividly remember getting the phone call and rushing to the hospital. It was a tough time in my life. Years later, my two younger brothers, who were home at the time of the incident, and I were talking about it, and to my surprise, they both were dealing with deep issues from our dad's death. They both blamed themselves for our dad dying.

I was completely unaware they had been blaming themselves for his death. They both felt that they should have done something differently, or should have done more. While they told me this, I thought to myself, "You two were 11 and 12 years old when it happened! What more could you have done?

After discussing this with my sister, she agreed with my brothers and also admitted having feelings of guilt and self-blame. She questioned whether she had done enough. Had she performed the compressions forcefully enough? Had she started them quickly enough? Could it have been her fault? These are the questions she had dwelled on for years.

I had no idea that my brothers and sister felt a sense of guilt for what had happened and held unforgiveness in their hearts. This unforgiveness was not unforgiveness for someone else, stemming from wondering whether someone else had done enough to save our father, but unforgiveness toward themselves for feeling they did not do enough.

I even questioned myself: not whether I could have done more to save him, since I was not there, but whether I could have been closer to him. Over the last few years of my dad's life, I had not had the relationship with him I would have liked to have had. He was the hardest-working man I knew.

He worked 6, if not 7, days a week for most of his life, refinishing rooms and doing interior and exterior painting of homes and buildings. As a teenager to make some money during the summer, I had helped him hang sheet rock on several of his jobs. It was not fun work.

My dad never once came home clean. He always worked hard and he was always dirty. The intense work ethic I have come from watching my dad work so hard his entire life.

My dad had a heart of gold. He would give you the shirt off his back if he saw you needed it. But, unfortunately, like so many other hard working people with hearts of gold, my dad had a drug problem.

At times, this prevented him from making decisions that could have been more beneficial to his life and to those around him. One year, our family did not have Christmas because my dad spent all of our money on drugs.

As a kid in middle school, I had to grow up quickly. My father, who was a great man, had a weak moment and gave in to peer-pressure, in turn becoming something no one ever expects to become, a crack addict. So, I had to become a man.

My family – my dad, my mom, and all 6 kids – went from living in a nice home with several acres of land for running and playing to living in a two-bedroom trailer behind my grandparents' house. I lived in a small one-room barn/shed that was about 12'x12' with no heating or air conditioning, roughly 50 yards from the house.

On several occasions, I remember my mom crying and upset, telling me to call my dad and tell him to come home to his family. This was difficult for me, at just 14 years of age. He was still my dad, and I loved him.

As I got a little older and was in the 11th grade, I moved away from home and moved in with a friend from school and his mother, who became like a second mother to me. After this, I saw my family as often possible, but I began to distance myself from the issues they still faced.

My dad, even with his drug addiction and the problems that come along with it, built and sold a home and moved to one of the homes I currently own. It is where he would take his last breath.

When he died, my mom wanted to know if he had been using drugs, because he had told her he wasn't. I am proud to say the blood test performed upon her request came back negative, showing no sign of drugs in his system.

So why did I question whether I could have had a closer relationship with my dad, and, did I blame my mom for that relationship not being as close as it could have been?

I remember my dad calling me on the phone one time, asking if I could come over and watch the mixed martial arts fights at the house with him on television and I told him I already had plans to watch them with some friends.

Another time, he called to see if I wanted to come over and play basketball with him, and I – being 21 at the time – told him "no" because I was again hanging out with friends.

I used to wonder if the distance between us was caused by my mom forcing me to call him and tell him to come home when he was out on a drug binge. Or, was it just the distance that develops in a typical father-son relationship when the son becomes an adult. Either way, I had unforgiveness in my heart for both myself and my mom.

If God forgives me, then it is only right that I forgive: forgive others and forgive myself. Forgiveness lets you heal. Forgiveness sets you free from the past while at the same time restoring the power you were once giving away. I forgave myself for questioning the relationship I had with my father.

I learned that continuing to ask those self-defeating questions was never going to give me the answers I desired. My dad was not going to come to me and tell me, "Yes, Danny. Our relationship was great, and I'm thankful for it."

He couldn't come back and tell me that. So, I had to forgive myself for feeling the way I felt and understand that I could not change the past. I could, however, appreciate and cherish the times we did have together. This is what I choose to focus on now.

So, instead of asking self-defeating questions, I now ask questions that will empower me and help me find the answers.

I also forgave my mom for the feelings I had towards her. No one gave her an instruction manual on how to handle the situation in which she found herself. She had done the best job she could do with the resources provided.

"There is no need to blame ourselves for situations and events that are beyond our control"

Danny Cole

Forgiveness equals healing. When someone does not heal, it causes him or her to live in a constant state of defeat. This state requires a person to carry a constant, life-crippling weight on his or her shoulders.

Given enough time, the weight from the unforgiveness will turn to bitterness, which will transform into anger, and then, like a black hole, it will swallow the unforgiving person whole, leaving nothing but an empty shell, void of life and filled with empty darkness.

When a person has reached this point, anger rises out of the pit of his or her soul whenever words or thoughts strike a nerve that governs whatever it is that holds power over that person. If this happens to you, it is a red flag, indicating that unforgiveness has power over you. In order to regain that power forgiveness needs to take place.

For most people, forgiving is easier said than done. Even though we know that if we do forgive, we will be released from torment's grasp and gain access into "Happy Land," our PRIDE steps in front of us and says, "Hey what are you doing? Don't you remember what just happened? They lied about you. They embarrassed you. They hurt you. Are you going to let them do that to you? You have a reason to be mad."

So now, because of pride, we rehearse the past experience and tighten our grip on bitterness and unforgiveness.

Pride is an ugly word and, unfortunately, pride stands in the way of forgiveness most of the time. Don't get me wrong. In the right context and state of mind, pride can help you excel.

Pride can make sure you complete the job or task perfectly because your name is on the line. Pride can cause you to work extra hard to make sure you repay debts. It can also create a sense of unity with a family, team, or country and cause you to carry yourself in a respectable manner.

Yet, for some people pride can be a weapon of destruction. It can destroy every area of your life. It can destroy your health, both mentally and physically. It can destroy your relationships. It can destroy your job. You must make sure you have a healthy dose of pride and not an overdose; otherwise, pride can destroy your life.

Pride can also cause you to relive negative past experiences. By reliving a past experience, your brain will also recreate the feelings that were felt at the time of the experience. If you recall an enjoyable memory, such as the birth of your first child, you will begin to smile and actually feel those emotions all over again.

You will feel the love and nervousness from holding your tiny bundle of joy in your arms for the first time. If you recall the memory of winning a competition, you will feel a burst of energy and actually feel your eyes grow brighter as the emotions of achievement and excitement wash over you.

On the other hand, if you recall the memory of a partner you loved and cared for more than anything in this world and this partner broke a promise to you.

A promise that meant equally as much to you as the person themselves, then feelings of frustration, disappointment, unworthiness, or betrayal are just some of the emotions that could come surging through your mind and body like a tidal wave. Flooding you with sadness and loneliness again and sending you back to that deep, dark hole of despair.

Be careful what you choose to recall. Your mind is powerful and will give you what you ask for. If you recall negative past experiences, you will feel negative emotions. If you recall positive past experiences, you will feel positive emotions. It's that simple. Do not complicate things.

If you are tired of feeling depressed and defeated, then change it. Start recalling positive past experiences instead reliving the negative ones and see what a difference it can make in your life. It is impossible to feel happy and sad at the same time. Depression and happiness cannot occupy the same place.

Your brain is your servant. It is your gift from God to create the life you believe you deserve. It is so powerful that it will elicit all the senses of your body from something imagined, just as it would from a real-life experience. That is the beauty of the gift you have been given.

If used with the right knowledge and understanding, it will serve you in the same manner it does for others who know "The Secret." It will guide you in the right direction and release you from past hurts and disappointments. The more you understand this, the more powerful you will be in life and the more you will attract to you your heart's desires.

When we forgive ourselves and forgive others, we break the chain of bondage and release the past. When we make the conscious effort to forgive, at that moment we stop giving our power away. We stop rehearsing painful past experiences that cannot be changed and begin to truly live in the now. The past is over. The present is all we have. Live it with POWER!

5 REASONS TO FORGIVE

1. Forgiveness does not equal condoning; it simply says, "I will not let the past control my future." If you continue to hold onto the past, your hands are closed to what the future has to give you.

2. Forgiveness is a sign of strength. Gandhi said, "The weak can never forgive. Forgiveness is an attribute of the strong."

3. When you forgive, you can heal; when you heal, you can grow. Forgiveness is a gift you give yourself. You may never forget, but you can heal, and when you heal, you are able to grow and become stronger and wiser.

4. Forgiveness is for you, not for them. When you hold on to unforgiveness and resentment, the only person it affects is you. You are the only person wasting all of your time and energy reliving the hurt, not someone else. Let go and have peace.

5. Because God forgives you. You and I sin on a daily basis. We were born into sin, and God sent Jesus Christ to die on the cross to pay the debt for our sins. If God can forgive us, then who are we to be unable to forgive ourselves or someone else?

Forgiveness releases you from the past and restores you mentally and physically. Studies have shown that forgiveness can lead to: higher self-esteem, healthier relationships, lowered blood pressure, less anxiety, increased spiritual awareness, and a stronger immune system.

Those who forgive also have fewer physical ailments such as; headaches, backaches, excessive weight loss, and upset stomach. When we release the grip on the past we can also release the grip of sickness.

Forgiveness is like a pleasant summer rain that comes and washes away all the pollen. What were once dirty and left marks everywhere you went is now bright, vibrant, and clean.

How to forgive

1. Realize that holding on to bitterness and unforgiveness does not harm the person who hurt you.

2. Know the best revenge is to live a happy and successful life.

3. Write down on a piece of paper the name of the person who has harmed you and the reason you forgive that person, and then throw that paper away.

4. Stop rehearsing the story.

5. Pray for the person who wronged you.

6. Understand that no one is perfect and that everyone makes mistakes.

7. Write down the good that came from the situation.

8. Know that your power is restored when you forgive.

9. Remember that the one who forgives is in control.

There has been much debate on whether you should tell a person who has harmed or hurt you that you have forgiven him or her. I do not feel that disclosing your forgiveness to someone with whom you have a grievance is paramount, unless that person has asked for your forgiveness.

If the situation is one in which the person had no idea he or she had upset you, there is nothing to be gained by informing that person of your forgiveness. Forgiveness is something you have to do for yourself. Do not be selfish and cause unneeded pain.

This is your life. Forgive and be happy, or hold on and be miserable. It's your choice.

It is your past

Do not be ashamed of your past.
It is your past.

Do not be embarrassed of your past.
It is your past.

Do not hold resentment from your past.
It is your past.

Do not let the past paint a false picture of who you
are today.Today is all we have. The past is gone.
It is your past.

Forgive and forget. You might not forget, but you
can forgive.
It is your past.

Notes

The second Key is Forgiveness. This Key will set you free from the past and enable you to enjoy the future.

<u>Positive Self-Image</u>

"Believe in yourself! Have faith in your abilities! Without a humble but reasonable confidence in your own powers you cannot be successful or happy."

Norman Vincent Peale

Do you know what the biggest problem plaguing this country is right now? Here is a little hint. This problem is far worse than the obesity issue, which is considered an epidemic, and even worse than the continually increasing national debt, which is currently over $17 trillion dollars.

Still not sure? Here, let me tell you. It is lack of self-confidence. Yep, that's right. Our perception of who we are as a person and what we believe about ourselves is the biggest problem plaguing this country today.

Your self-image is directly related to your self-esteem which is extremely important for you on a conscious and subconscious level for excelling and being happy in all areas of life. The definition of self-esteem is confidence in one's own worth or abilities; self-respect. This is one of the most important keys that will unlock the door of endless opportunities for you.

It is unfortunate, but most people today lack confidence in

their own personal abilities. This shortage of confidence causes most people to question their ability in having a strong lasting relationship, to be a good mother or father, to be financially stable, to be happy, or successful.

The lack of self-confidence isn't always easily visible, but when it's there, it turns any decision making process into an extremely difficult task. Lack of self-confidence only creates a massive amount of stress and worry to any situation.

This extra stress and worry only causes someone to repeatedly second guess themselves, often making them feel as if they are going crazy. It can also cause some to even put off making a decision all together. And what is the internal reward for not taking action?

They are internally rewarded by becoming frustrated and angry at themselves. By not making decisions people are not in control of their lives. By not making decisions they are letting life happen instead of making life happen.

I'm sure on a daily basis that you yourself encounter someone who is inhibited from enjoying their life to the fullest due to the lack of self-confidence. You can see it on their face and in the way they carry themselves. They just look beat down by life. They don't have that "pep" in their step. They are not wearing a happy carefree smile on their face, only lines of past worries and doubt.

Some people try to hide their lack of self-confidence by appearing to be "perfect". Some make sure they are dressed impeccably without a single hair out of place while others might have the cleanest house you have ever seen. Others may even act overly "tough" on the outside to keep people at bay while on the inside they are nervous someone will uncover the truth - the truth that they are filled with insecurity.

By not having a healthy positive self-image you are only weighing yourself down, making life difficult. Having a poor self-image is like carrying an anchor with you. It may not be that difficult at first but, the longer you carry it with you the less distance you will travel. You will eventually only grow tired and weary and just become stuck!

"Do not be afraid of your failures, learn from them."

Richard Branson

Having a poor self-image and low self-esteem will trigger different actions in different people. Some may overeat, due to mental or physical abuse as a child, to cope with low self-esteem causing weight gain and other possible illnesses such as diabetes and high blood pressure. While others, may shop continuously to fill the void of a poor self-image from not being shown how to handle money properly and putting themselves deeper and deeper into debt.

Whether it is shopping, eating or any other action that is triggered, it momentarily gives a feeling of being in control. At that moment the person may not be in control of how they feel about themselves but, they are INSTANTLY in control of who decides if they overeat or not, THEM! They are instantly in control of who makes the decision if they make that purchase or not. Them! No one else. The dark lie of instant gratification is the illusion of being in control.

You are blessed with the Infinite Mind of God and it is working through you to create your reality. But having a poor self-image will only diminish the confidence you have in your abilities which affects the reality you are capable of creating. Having a poor self-image and lack of self-confidence is horrible, dis-empowering, and detrimental to you living the life you deserve.

This is your life! You deserve to have everything that is good and grand in it! It is your natural God given birth right to be blessed. A poor self-image and low self-esteem can slowly stop blessings from the Universe from coming to you.

"Most fears of rejection rest on the desire from approval from other people. Don't base your self-esteem on their opinions."

Harvey Mackay

I've had several jobs in my thirty-six years of existence. I've done everything from working at fast food restaurants, being a landscaper, real estate agent, car salesman, gym manager, yoga instructor, to life coaching and motivational speaking and on a daily basis I encountered and still encounter people from all walks of life who suffer with insecurities.

Insecurities are unbiased. They will relentlessly attack any and every one they can regardless of religion, ethnic group, age or social status. These life stealing thieves could inhabit only one area of a person's life to encompassing ALL areas of their life.

Insecurities can include everything from being insecure about: age, weight, sexuality, height, intelligence, relationships, worthiness, money, career, and body - just to name a few. What I have found in my studies is having insecurities is a catalyst for creating low self-esteem.

Mike, a husband and father of three with one on the way, told me he wanted the better paying IT position at his job that just became available.

He said with the new position he could provide for his family effortlessly due to the thirty percent raise in pay. He said it also required fewer hours and allowed him to work from home. But, he expressed to me he was insecure about his abilities in that position and wasn't sure he would apply, even though he was over qualified for it.

Sarah always excelled in academics. For her it just came easy. She graduated with a 3.8 grade point average with little effort. After taking a year off from school she told me she wanted to go back to further her education in the field of radiology, but did not feel smart enough.

She felt that because she took a year break she had forgotten everything and everyone else was going to be ahead of her.

John married his high school sweetheart. He has been married for seven years and loves his wife with all his heart but had one issue he never brought up to her. He didn't feel respected by his wife. She never took his feelings into consideration and made all the major decisions without his input.

He told me he wanted respect in their marriage, but was scared to ask for it. He said, "It is hard to ask for respect when you don't respect yourself."

These three people you just read about all have a similar trait in common. Do you know what that trait is? They are all MISSING OUT ON LIFE! Just like everyone else with insecurities and low self-esteem.

These people want more and you know what? They deserve more. But, unfortunately, they go on wearing that old ugly coat of defeat. They are imprisoned by it. They continue living their lives in shackles. But, did you know that that old ugly coat of defeat can be taken off, forever? And, it can be replaced with a brand new, perfectly fitting tailor made suit of success and happiness!

It all starts with our self-image. The psychiatrist Karl Menniger said, "Attitudes are more important than facts." While in the car business as a salesman, we had a saying that was very similar, it was, "Fake it till you make it." Believe you are great until you become great.

Your attitude about yourself and what you think about yourself is far more important than what or how others think about you. It doesn't matter what struggles you faced in the past or the insecurities you may have now, all that matters is what you believe about yourself.

Once you change what you think about yourself and what you believe about yourself you will begin to see changes in your mood and your life. Your thoughts and beliefs will paint the picture for your emotions to act out. What you believe about yourself is sure to manifest in your life.

Our self-image is created and developed over time through interactions and experiences we have with our parents, friends, teachers, peers, even things we see and hear on the radio and television. Whether they were positive or negative, or whether we perceived them as positive or negative, and especially how we applied them to ourselves, determined how we felt and currently feel about ourselves today.

If we heard a constant assault on our physical appearance due to being overweight then that could lead to becoming extremely introverted and not wanting to be seen in public.

But, on the other hand, if we were told how attractive we were and how our sense of style was "cool" then it could have a completely different outcome. It could cause the feelings of confidence and self-worth which could make being seen in public and meeting new people a pleasurable experience.

If we had the misfortune of being called stupid or dumb and had our intelligence questioned, then finding the courage to respond to questions in public or a group setting such as a meeting or even a night out with friends enjoying a game of trivia would be next to impossible.

But if we had our teachers and parents constantly boosting our self-esteem by telling us what a great job we are doing and how we learn so fast and easily, then speaking in front of crowds could possibly be a lot easier and more enjoyable.

The feelings that were created are attached to the image we hold of ourselves and will determine the actions we take later in life. Norman Vincent Peale wrote in his book, *The Power of Positive Thinking*, "All of your actions, feelings, behavior, and even your abilities are always constant with this self-image."

Your self-image will determine the outcome of your life. It will determine how others treat you. Your self-image will determine the amount of money or happiness you will have in life. It will also determine your worthiness.

You can say all day long that you desire something but, if you do not believe you deserve it then you will not get it. If you want to be treated with respect but deep down do not feel you deserve it, then guess what? You will not get respect.

You can say all day long you want to earn $100,000 a year but if you do not believe you can make that much money, then guess what? You will not earn $100,000 a year. If you want to be happy but do not feel you can be happy, then guess what? You will not be happy. You will not receive what you do not believe you will receive.

The Bible says, "*According to your faith it shall be given to you.*" So, with this being said, you have to be careful what and who you listen to. You will begin to believe what you see and hear on a consistent basis.

Say for instance, if you are around someone who is struggling financially and they are constantly telling you how bad the economy is and that there is no way to earn extra money. Over time you will eventually believe it due to the fact they are consistently reinforcing this thought with their "acts" and their "facts."

But, if you did a little research you would find that according to the Boston Consulting Group's study in 2014, the United States had 7,135,000 millionaire households. A huge increase compared to the previous year's study done by Wealthsight showing only 5,231,000 millionaire US households.

From the things you watch to those whom you associate with you will hear and see their thoughts and beliefs on a consistent basis. If it is negative then tune it out. It does not matter the source it is coming from because, if you are told something enough times you will eventually believe it. Remember the Law of Attraction, if you think it you will bring it. Do not bring negativity into your life by thinking the wrong things.

You may have to stop watching certain television shows or types of movies to achieve this. You may also have to select a new group of friends that will better suit your developing mind and life. It may be family members you have to keep distance from, at least for a short period, while you build your self-image. It may even be your best friend.

Whatever the source of negativity stems from; music, television, movies, or friends, if it is negative then tune it out. Carefully select what you choose to view because those are the images that will be stored in your mind forever. And remember to choose who you associate with wisely because you will eventually become the company you keep.

Positive Self-Image

"No one can make you feel inferior without your consent."

Eleanor Roosevelt

I began to learn, as a young kid, how to ignore the painful comments of my peers. I'm sure if they knew what the comments they spewed at me would do to my young and vulnerable self-image they would have re-framed, but the sabotage to my developing self-esteem had already taken place

I have a hereditary trait that was passed down to me from my mom, which was passed down from her mom. My right eye is very weak and it will turn in, especially if I am tired or stressed out.

Growing up, other kids always teased me about it. They would say things like "who are you looking at!," "How many fingers am I holding up," or calling me cross-eyed. It was a constant beating of words that damaged my self-esteem for a long time. Because of it, I didn't like looking anyone in their eyes and avoided it if at all possible.

I remember my mom dropping me off at my buddy Bill's house and meeting his mom Connie and her boyfriend Tim, for the first time. It was a beautiful sunny fall morning and my mom pulled down the short driveway just off the main road to their smaller, but nice, brick home. I jumped out of the car and walked across the thick green grass to the front door.

I was excited and nervous all at the same time. Bill was my best friend at the time and I was looking forward to hanging out with him and staying up late playing, but I was also nervous because I was only thirteen and my confidence in meeting new people was low. It was battered and bruised due to cruel remarks from other kids about my eye and other physical attributes like a larger nose and "buck" teeth.

I balled my little sweaty hand into a fist and knocked on the door and Connie and Tim opened the large white door and greeted me with a hand shake and a warm smile. I shook their hand and just stared down at the ground so they wouldn't notice my eye, just in case it was turned in at all. After what felt like an eternity, Bill finally showed up and saved me from the awkward moment, and we ran off to his room to play some video games.

Later that night I asked Bill what his mom and Tim thought about me, but I was not ready for the response I was about to receive. He told me that his mom liked me but Tim didn't.

I was confused and my feelings were a little hurt too because, how could he not like me? He didn't even know me. "What did I do wrong," I thought. My mom raised me not to steal, not lie, and to be respectful. My mom would have given me a severe butt whoopin if I went against the way she raised me, and she had a way of knowing if I did anything wrong, even if no one told her, so I knew better.

He told me the reason Tim didn't like me was because I did not look him in the eyes when I met him and to him that was a sign of not being trustworthy.

That blew me away. I didn't know what to think. I got made fun of because of my weak eye turning in so I didn't like looking people in the eyes and now I had an adult who didn't like me because I didn't look him in the eyes.

What now? What was I supposed to do? Look people in the eyes and have them make fun of me or not look them in the eyes and have them possibly not like me and think I couldn't be trusted? I was one confused kid.

As I grew older I accepted the fact that I had flaws. No one is perfect and these flaws are what make me unique. And once I grew more confident in myself I didn't even look at them as flaws anymore. I just accepted them for what they were, me. If I am confident in myself then no one can hurt me with stares or words. Words only have power to hurt you if you allow them to.

"Wanting to be someone else is a waste of the person you are."

Marilyn Monroe

What causes low self-esteem?

There are a number of contributing factors to low self-esteem and insecurities. More often than not, the lack of self-confidence stems from insecurities of the past that were carried to the present. Due to the carrying over of insecurities your future will be negatively affected. We will now take a look at a few of the reasons for low self-esteem here.

Unrealistic Expectations

Often times parents, other adults, or mentors have very high expectations of others. If these expectations are not met, whether the expectation was realistic or not, unfulfillment and failure can dominate their thoughts. They feel worthless or "just not good enough" since they were unable to obtain the goal for them and let them down.

Comparing Yourself to Others

If you constantly compare yourself to others in areas where you are not as dominate then you will only set yourself up to be let down. If you constantly compare yourself academically to the person who always excels and you don't then you will not feel good about yourself.

If you are constantly comparing yourself to those people in "beauty" magazines you will be let down. They have personal trainers and chefs and have been airbrushed for the magazines. "Beauty" magazines only make you feel ugly. You are beautiful the way you are. The only person you should compare yourself to is the person you were yesterday.

Abuse

Whether it was mental, physical, or both, a person will carry feelings of inadequacy and feeling like they deserve to be used and punished for being themselves. Abuse can cause a person to be extremely submissive or overly disruptive and abusive. It can also cause some to develop eating disorders to cope with the feelings.

Appearance

People often times will feel inferior when they compare themselves to models or other people who they feel are attractive. They will look at a physical attribute someone else has whether it is: nose, eyes, hair, body shape, ears hands, face, etc. and wish they had it or looked like someone else.

Often times self-esteem is damaged due to putting acceptance in materialistic items. Believing that if he or she is not wearing the "in" style fashion or driving the right car and so forth, then they are an outsider and not worthy of value.

Repeatedly Criticized

When a person is constantly reminded they are not as good as someone else or they are not good at something they will have a decrease in self-confidence. This can lead them to not participate in anything for fear of being criticized.

Neglect

Not having parents or others you care about show they care for you. Everyone needs acceptance, attention, and love and when they do not receive it they feel insignificant. When they are involved in something they are passionate about and no one is there to support them, the feelings of being alone and unworthy begin to settle in. Trust is hard to gain once this happens due to the fact they do not want to feel abandoned again.

Unfaithfulness

Having someone, whether it is a friend or romantic partner, lie and betray the bond of trust or cheat can cause a person to question their worthiness. It can cause them to question if they are flawed and even if they are capable of being loved.

Negative Self Talk

If the thought pattern carried on within your head is negative then it only reinforces that negative thought. A consistently reinforced thought can only and will be transformed into a belief. Once the thought is a belief your subconscious will create the behavior to match. So be careful of things such as; I am dumb, I am ugly, I am fat, I am worthless. The words "I AM" have the power to create your self-image accordingly.

Common Characteristics of Someone with Low Self-Esteem/Poor Self-Image:

They have higher levels of anxiety.

They have a tendency to withdraw from social settings or group activities.

They tend to attract the wrong relationships.

They tend to have hurtful and volatile relationships.

They have a constant internal dialogue of negativity.

They always expect the worst.

They doubt their abilities.

They are extra sensitive to criticism.

They are quick tempered.

They will dismiss positive feedback.

They often think others perceive them negatively.

They are extreme people pleasers.

They abuse alcohol or other drugs.

They never finish projects.

They constantly need approval.

They cannot be alone.

They have eating disorders.

They overly exercise or workout.

They take everything personal.

They are self-centered.

They are expert excuse makers.

*"You have been criticizing yourself for years, and it hasn't worked.
Try approving of yourself and see what happens."*

Louise L. Hay

Building your Self-Image

Let's consciously create a positive self-image. One that will give you the confidence to live the life you deserve.

 Why would you want to have a positive self-image? I'm glad you asked. Other than the reasons you are probably thinking of right now, research has shown individuals with a positive self-image have a better overall quality of life.

Those with a positive self-image are healthier mentally and physically and have stronger relationships. They have a greater sense of inner peace, feel better about the decisions they make, and feel more attractive. In essence, life will be more fun, enjoyable, and successful if you have a positive self-image.

There are several ways to build your self-image and increase your level of confidence. Here are a few of those ways:

Take a self-esteem/ image inventory. The only way to improve on something is to know where there needs to be improvement. Grab a journal. If you don't have a journal then a piece of paper and any writing instrument will do. Draw a line down the center of the page. Title the left column STRENGTHS and on the right column title it WEAKNESSES.

Now that you have that done, write down 10 strengths and 10 weaknesses under the appropriate column. This may be easier for some than others. If you can't think of any strengths then recall a time when someone complimented you on something. Maybe someone complimented you on being pretty, a great listener, a well-dresser, creative, good with money, whatever the compliment was, write it down.

Everyone has strengths. EVERYONE. Once the list is made look at the weaknesses and realize no one is perfect and only see them as areas of improvement. Now look at the strengths column and smile. These are your strengths.

Keep a daily journal of self-image improvements and achievements. These could be words spoken to or thought about you, actions done for someone, etc. By keeping a journal of the daily achievements you will reinforce the belief that you are improving on. You will reinforce the belief you desire to have. Just as experiences reinforced you to believe negatively about yourself then experiences will also reinforce the positive you believe about yourself.

Visualize yourself being the person you want to be. By picturing yourself being; confident, receiving the promotion at work, being happy, feeling attractive, or whatever it is you want, you are sending the image to your subconscious mind, and it must create what is shown. Visualize with as much of your emotions as possible. Really feel and believe you are what you visualize. The stronger your emotions are the easier it will be to create the new belief.

Surround yourself with positive people. If you are around positive people then you will be in the presence of positive vibes and soon you, yourself, can resonate with those positive vibes. Avoid people, situations, and places that are negative. If you don't, you will begin to resonate with the vibes being sent out and attract the same in return.

Avoid those people who are throwing insults at you. A common situation among those with low self-esteem is hanging out with crowds that degrade them or take advantage of them, and put up with it, in hopes one day to receive approval from the group. If you don't value yourself, no one else will.

Do not compare yourself to others. Everyone has their own STRENGTHS and weaknesses. By comparing yourself to others who have strengths where you have weaknesses is a waste of time and can only lower your self-confidence. And it is done intentionally, by you. Why would you make your own self feel bad? You are you. Just be a better person today than you were yesterday.

Do something for others. Doing something for others is selfless and will make the recipient feel good. We as human beings always feel good when someone is happy from something *we* have done for them.

Instead of trying to achieve perfection focus on accomplishments and achievements. No one is perfect physically or at performing tasks. If there is a person you feel is perfect, chances are they do not feel perfect about themselves. If you focus on your accomplishments and achievements then you will continue to grow and build your belief in yourself and your abilities.

Set realistic expectations; don't set yourself up for failure. If you set expectations that are unable to be met you will only let yourself down and lower your self-esteem and view yourself as a failure. Set goals you can achieve. The larger goals should be broken down into smaller more attainable goals.

Smile. People smile when they are happy. By smiling your mind will believe you are happy, even if you're not, and start to create those feelings of happiness inside of you.

I remember hearing Anthony Robbins talk about an experiment that was conducted by the University of California on manic depressants. All the residents at this particular facility were manic depressants and have all tried the typical forms of treatment for the disorder, but were still in this unfortunate state.

For the experiment they were asked to try something different. They were asked to smile. No other medications. No other counseling. Just smile. They were told to smile as much as they could for as long as they could. Over the course of the experiment, everyone who participated began to smile more regularly and for longer periods of time.

At the end of the month, those who fully participated in the experiment were cured from manic depression and were able to leave the facility. *Smiling sends signals to your brain that you are happy thus causing a state of happiness.*

Write 10 things you like about yourself daily. Grab your journal and write 10 things you like about yourself. It could be your smile, your nose, you have pretty eyes, you are a great listener, whatever it is you like about yourself. This will reinforce your ideas and make them beliefs. Do this at night time before bed.

Dress in the style of clothes that make you feel good. By dressing the way you want and the way that makes you feel good creates the feelings of confidence and being happy within you and you will project them on the outside of you as well. Feel confident in your style of dress.

Do things that interest you. Do not do things just because everyone else is doing them. By only doing what others want you can lose your own identity. Involve yourself in the things that interest you. If bowling, hiking, or writing interest you then do them. Discover your interest and enjoy them.

Read something inspirational daily. By reading something inspirational you set yourself into motion for positive vibes to be sent out and to return back to you. Something you read could possibly inspire you to change your life or someone's around you.

Exercise regularly. Exercising on a regular basis will change the physical appearance of your body to a more slimmer and toner you. It will lower your body fat percentage, it can also lower blood pressure, and at the same time will release the "feel good" chemical of endorphins in your brain that cause you to experience stress relief and feel happier. Daily exercise is one of the most single best options to improve self-esteem.

A friend told me a story he heard about Buddha. Now Buddha is a very wise, peaceful and spiritual man. One day, upon hearing how great, wise and how happy Buddha was, a man unhappy with his own life, decided he wanted to prove Buddha a fraud.

He said to himself that no one could be that happy with their life. No one could be so happy and content with their life that they are completely at peace and no one could cause them to become angry. So, he set out on his journey and he traveled thousands of miles to reach this "enlightened" man.

When he finally arrived at his destination and Buddha was only a few yards away from him, he grinned and could not wait to prove Buddha and the world wrong. He walked over quickly and, with each step, the man grew angrier and more intent on doing what he set out to do.

When he was finally in front of Buddha he began to curse Buddha. He called him and his family any and everything he could think of. The man told Buddha that he was a fraud and that no one believes in him and his teachings are pathetic.

Buddha looked up to the man and simply and quietly said, "Can I ask you a question?" The man said sternly, "yeah, sure go ahead!" Buddha proceeded, "If someone tries to give you a gift and you do not accept it, then whose gift is it?" The man replied rudely, "Well, the person who tried to give it to you." Buddha said, "Exactly" smiled and turned around.

We do not have to accept gifts from other people. If they are offering you a gift whose sole purpose is to cause you pain, then do not accept it. If you do not accept it then it has no power. The only way a gift of negativity has power is if we give it power and that is by accepting it.

It is not yours to receive and hold on to anyway. You do not deserve the gift of negativity in any way, shape, or fashion. So, do not accept it. You deserve nothing but the best in all areas of your life. So act like it.

I want to leave you with 1 Easy Trick to build self-confidence. This easy trick is something I have been using with my clients for years with great results.

The 3 *R* Technique

"Realize, Reject, and Replace"

We have about 60,000 thoughts in a day. That is a tremendous amount of thoughts, isn't it? The problem with most of those thoughts is they are the same thoughts we had yesterday!

To get different results we have to have different thoughts. Or as Albert Einstein said, "We cannot solve our problems with the same thinking we used when we created them." If you are thinking negatively about yourself you are going to feel negatively about yourself and in essence attract negativity to your life. Like a magnet you will attract to you what you believe you are.

So, you have to change your habitual thought pattern to that of a positive thought pattern in order to feel positive about yourself and attract positive situations and circumstances to your life. Not to mention, you need to do it to feel good about yourself on a constant basis. And isn't that what everyone wants anyway, to feel good about ourselves?

The neat and powerful thing about the human mind is we can only have one thought at a time. That's right, out of all the 60,000 thoughts we have in a day, from what are we going to eat for breakfast, what to wear, the traffic, lunch, dinner, work, chores, the kids, friends, the significant other, laundry and everything else, we can only entertain one thought at a time.

The reason this is so great is because you can also only have one emotion at a time. That's right, only one emotion at a time. The thought we have will dictate the emotion we have. And in return, the emotion we have will dictate the action we take.

So, if you are having negative thoughts it will be impossible for you to feel good, positive, or happy. Only negative. And, on the same token, if you are having positive thoughts it will be impossible to feel sad. Don't believe me? Go ahead and give it a try. Think of something that makes you happy and excited and see if you can be upset or depressed. Depression and Happiness cannot occupy the same space at the same time.

So, here is the trick. Once you **REALIZE** you are having a negative thought, automatically **REJECT** it and then **REPLACE** it, with a thought of power or a thought that brings you happiness and joy. Because remember, negative thoughts equal negative emotions, and negative emotions equal negative actions. Positive thoughts equal positive emotions and positive emotions equal positive actions.

If it is a negative thought you are having yourself, as soon as you *Realize* it you should immediately *Reject* it and *Replace* it with a strong positive thought. Replace it with something such as; an accomplishment, of you winning a competition, or of you helping others, or being with a loved one. Think of something that makes you feel strong and powerful, confident, or happy.

Reject the negative thought and Replace it with the strong, powerful, confident, or happy one and watch the immediate difference in the way you will feel. You will change your state instantly. You will go from feeling down in the dumps to seeing your head lift up, eyes getting brighter, chest out, and feeling better all in the blink of an eye.

This simple trick will do wonders to build a power self-esteem and train your habitual thought pattern to work for you instead of against you. The American Philosopher and psychologist William James said, "The greatest discovery of my generation is that human beings can alter their lives by altering of their minds." Remember, your thoughts determine your emotions, your emotions determine your actions, and your actions determine your destiny.

Notes

The third Key is A Positive Self-Image. With this key you can unlock the true you. You can be the person you want to be, not what someone else said you were.

Gratitude

"The power, the wisdom, the creativity of the universe - you open the door through gratitude."

Deepak Chopra

As the famous motivational guru Zig Ziglar often said, "You must have an attitude of gratitude." Gratitude is one of the most important key principles in the formula for success and happiness. Withholding gratitude is the equivalent of having a dam in the middle of a powerful river. The water wants to flow freely but can't due to the blockage. Remove the blockage and let the river of abundance flow freely in your life.

Have an Attitude of Gratitude

Think about this for a moment. If you are not grateful for what you have, then why should you be given more?

The moving, eye-opening story you are about to read is one that my good friend James told me about him and his son, Austin. Austin is a blonde-haired, blue-eyed little six-year-old with a heart of gold. He is the apple of his daddy's eye.

This short story is in James' words about the time his son learned about the powerful principle of Gratitude.

"One particular weekend, Austin and I were extremely busy. We had two birthday parties to attend and had to purchase the gifts as well as some refreshments. All at last minute, of course, but, what do you expect? I'm a guy; I'm always doing things last minute. While inside one of the many stores that day, Austin found and was playing with a little bright red car that had flames running down the side, and asked me to buy it for him. His behavior was exceptionally well, especially considering all the running around we had to do, and I love him, so I bought it for him.

He was running his new little car over all the clothes and chairs we passed by, and had it doing flips and turns in the air like one of those acrobatic airplanes. He was thoroughly enjoying it. When we left, we had just one last store to go into. While there, he located the toy section very quickly, the reason I know this is because in no time he came running up to me with a big smile on his cute little face holding another toy he wanted.

He said, "Dad! Look at this toy! I want it!" I told him that I just bought him a toy at the last store and without missing a beat and told me, "I know, but we can sell that one, I like this one better."

After briefly laughing to myself, because if you knew Austin, you would know he loves having yard sales and will sell anything and everything he can get his hands on. He is a true salesman, just like his dad. I looked him in the eyes and told him that I was not going to buy it for him.

He was a little upset, as I expected him to be, and once we finished up inside the store, we walked to the car.

After he buckled his seatbelt, he looked at me with his big blue eyes and asked, "Dad, why would you not get me that toy I wanted?" So we had a little talk about gratitude. I asked him, "Son, if you didn't appreciate the first toy I bought you, then why should I buy you another one?"

Then I continued the conversation by asking him, "Do you know that there are other children all over the world that do not even have toys? There are a lot of children in the world that are unable to have a lot of the things you enjoy on a daily basis." I smiled and rubbed his little blonde head and told him he needs to be thankful for what he has. He smiled and shook his head and said, "Yes sir, I understand."

A few months later we were out running errands again, and he asked me to buy him a spider man costume. He loved Spider Man and saw the costume was on sale for only $15. While showing me the costume, he made sure he told me it was on sale, because he knows I like deals. So, I bought it for him. Once we were finished there, we went to the final store of the day.

While at the last store, what do you think happened? Yep, he located the toy section again, but this time it was different. He ran up to me, "Dad, I don't want you to buy this because I love my spider man costume but isn't it cool!"

It was one of those Nerf footballs that creates a whistling sound when you throw it. "Dad, we could have a lot of fun with that football couldn't we?" I told him yes and then he smiled and spun around. I watched his little blonde head bob back and forth as he tossed the football into the air and catching it again as he made his way to the toy section to return the ball.

Now, what do you think we walked out of that store with? You guessed it; that cool Nerf football that whistles when you throw it. And yes, we did have a lot of fun with it. Now, either he learned about gratitude or he was a heck of a salesman at a very young age. I'm sure it's gratitude, because after our little conversation we had in the car about gratitude, he made sure he told me all the time how thankful he was for everything."

If James blessed his son with the means he had when his son showed gratitude, then think how much more God can do for us with HIS means when we are grateful. God is Infinite Power and has unlimited resources.

He wants to bless us. He is just waiting to bless each and every one of us when, like James blessed his son, we are good and have the spirit of gratitude.

What exactly is gratitude? Gratitude is simply defined as the quality of being thankful and the readiness to show appreciation for and to return kindness. It sounds simple enough, doesn't it? To be grateful is to show appreciation for what you have or what you have been given and to return kindness. Unfortunately, for some this simple principle has been lost and forgotten or in some cases never taught.

If you do not possess this key, success is going to be just out of reach for you. You will continue to thirst for more, never being fulfilled. This thirst will not be quenched until you are happy with what you already have and show appreciation for it.

If you do not have gratitude, happiness will also be missing from your life. If you are unhappy with what you have now, then you will not be happy with what you obtain in the future. If you are not happy with who you are now, then you will not be happy with who you become.

Possessing this Key will open the door of abundance from the Universe and allow it to flow to you instead of you ceaselessly chasing after it.

Having all the money and success only changes the outside circumstances. If you are not first, fulfilled and happy on the inside, none of it matters.

Brad Pitt is world famous and known for his good looks as well as being a talented actor and producer. According to most of the world's standards it would appear he has it all; good looks, fortune, fame, a beautiful wife, and a loving family. In an interview with Rolling Stone magazine, he had this to say. "I'm telling you, once you've got everything, then you're just left with yourself. I've said it before and I'll say it again: it doesn't help you sleep any better, and you don't wake up any better because of it."

It doesn't matter who you are or what you have; if you are not first happy on the inside and grateful for what you have, then you can gain everything underneath the sun and you will still not be satisfied. If your spirit is empty and unhappy, tangible possessions will not quench the thirst.

Now, I'm not saying Brad Pitt is not grateful or unhappy. I don't know Brad and have not had the luxury to speak with him, but I do know that even with all of the "things" he has accrued, like so many others, he still has that empty feeling inside.

"Be thankful for what you have; you'll end up having more. If you concentrate on what you don't have, you will never, ever have enough"

Oprah Winfrey

Ungrateful

There are two reasons that someone might be ungrateful. The first reason someone may feel ungrateful is because they live in the mental state of "entitlement." Those in the mental state of entitlement feel everyone owes them something. This type of person gets angry when things are not done for them or they are not given what they want.

They take no responsibility for the situation they are in. Those residing in the "entitlement" group are unknowingly powerless. They relinquish the right to their power of Gratitude and the blessings it brings the moment they are ungrateful and start thinking others owe them something.

The second reason people might feel ungrateful is that they are confused. What I mean by this is that some people feel they do not deserve to be happy or successful, because of a negative situation that caused psychological pain. This negative experience could have either happened *to* them, or *by* them. The experience could involve actions or words. But now, they are stuck rehearsing the incident over and over and can't forgive themselves.

Because of this situation that happened in the past, these people feel a deep conviction to punish themselves. They feel being depressed or living in a constant state of defeat is how they can right the wrong they committed. Why do they feel this way? That is a good question. It's because they are withholding something extremely important from themselves: self-forgiveness.

When forgiveness is not allowed, all too often allowing oneself to find anything to be grateful for is out of the question. People living in this state are overwhelmed with negative emotions and feel stuck, and believe they deserve to feel this way. It's a sad state to be in.

What has to be realized is that the past is gone. There is nothing we can do about it. The future is not here and it is not promised. Today is here and it is all that we have, so make the most of it. Forgive and begin to see the things to be grateful for. Once you begin, your life will change for the better.

It is easy for most people to give thanks in the good times, but it is essential in the bad times. When we begin to notice the "silver lining" in the situation, the situation doesn't look so dire any longer. Being grateful gives us power and also brings us more things to be grateful about.

The Bible says in 1 Thessalonians 5:18, *"Be joyful always, pray continually, and give thanks in all you do for this is God's will for you in Christ Jesus."* If we are grateful, it will bring us closer to God, The Infinite Power. The closer we are to the source, the stronger and more powerful we are.

Benefits of Gratitude. The benefits of gratitude have been studied by scientists, doctors, and professionals across the globe. Here is a graph from Happierhuman.com from their article "The 31 Benefits of Gratitude you didn't know about: "How Gratitude can change your life" by Amit Amin. The graph shows the benefits of Gratitude.

Gratitude

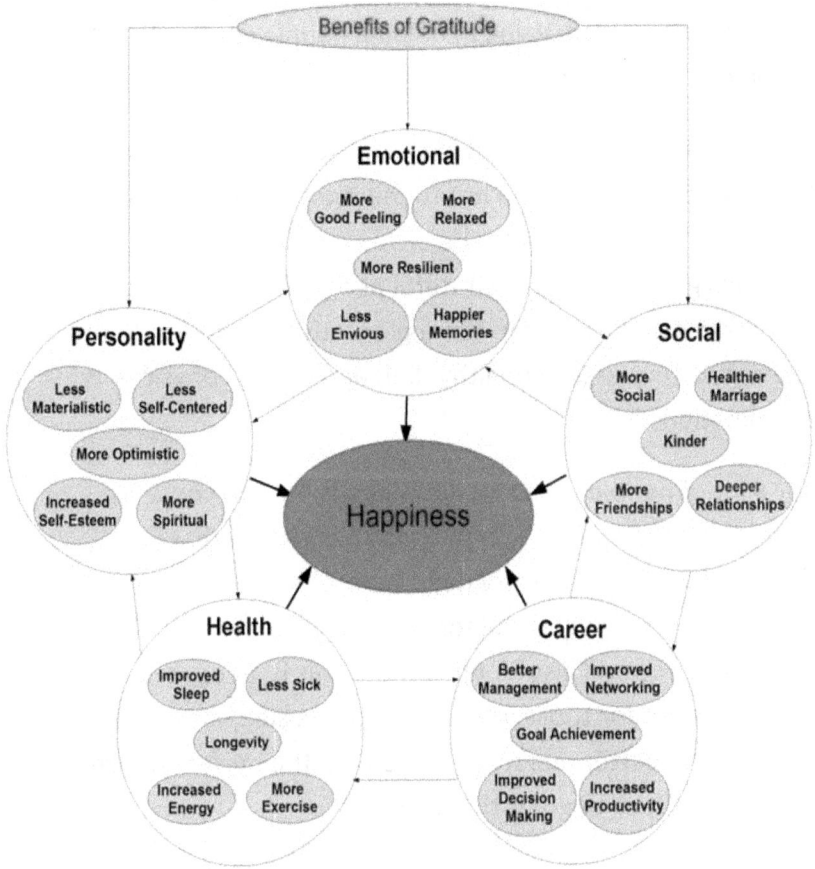

Benefits of Gratitude

Emotional
- More Good Feeling
- More Relaxed
- More Resilient
- Less Envious
- Happier Memories

Personality
- Less Materialistic
- Less Self-Centered
- More Optimistic
- Increased Self-Esteem
- More Spiritual

Social
- More Social
- Healthier Marriage
- Kinder
- More Friendships
- Deeper Relationships

Health
- Improved Sleep
- Less Sick
- Longevity
- Increased Energy
- More Exercise

Career
- Better Management
- Improved Networking
- Goal Achievement
- Improved Decision Making
- Increased Productivity

Happiness

According to Dr. Robert A. Emmons, "Gratitude research is beginning to suggest that feelings of thankfulness have tremendous positive value in helping people cope with daily problems, especially stress."

Those that live in a constant state of Gratitude always seem to have, to be happy, and not to mention are a lot easier to be around than those who are always complaining. Dr. Emmons goes on to say, "Grateful people take better care of themselves and engage in more protective health behaviors like regular exercise, a healthy diet, and regular physical examinations."

For a lot of people, good quality sleep is hard to come by. Research done by *Psychology Today* has shown that by taking a few minutes every night before bed to jot down a few things you are grateful for, you will not only fall asleep faster, but you will also sleep longer. This is an especially great exercise for those who have trouble sleeping or falling asleep. The better quality sleep you get the better chance you have at feeling great the next day.

There are many ways to strengthen a relationship, and numerous studies have shown that expressing gratitude for the small things your partner does will significantly strengthen your relationship. This requires a heartfelt, sincere verbal acknowledgement of something you're grateful for that your partner does or has done.

Good health is a priority in many people's lives today. A simple way to improve your health without hitting the gym is to incorporate gratitude in your daily routine. Optimism is a result of gratefulness, and optimism, according to *WebMD,* is linked to a healthier immune system. And for those of you that are in school, being grateful is also linked to higher GPAs.

Being grateful has been proven to increase the quality of your health by improving your sleep, boosting your immune system, and increasing your energy levels. Being grateful increases the quality of your career by improving your decision-making, goal achievement, and by making you a better manager.

Being grateful increases the quality of your social life by creating deeper relationships, being friendlier, and more social. These are only a few areas and positive benefits of the power of gratitude.

I know it's hard to feel happy and optimistic when everything you are shown and told is doom and gloom. You can't turn on the television today without a series of negative stories being forced in your face. With this constant bombardment of violence, the downed economy, and corrupt politicians coming from every media source available, combined with the normal everyday stresses of life, it's no wonder anxiety and depression seems so common place and "normal."

Everyone in life has experienced turmoil of some sort, you and I included. No one is immune to a negative occurrence once in a while, but I have sadly heard some people say, "I don't have anything to be grateful for." This is simply a false statement. Everyone has something to be grateful for. Everyone. Even if it is only waking up today to have the opportunity to better your life, everyone has something to be grateful for.

Usually, after a few moments with those who say they have nothing to be thankful for, and asking a couple of questions, they begin to go down a list of tangible items they do have to be thankful for. The list ranges from things such as the shoes on their feet, to the iPad they have, to the car they drive, to the intangible things such as being creative, or having the ability to sing, or to make others laugh, or just being a good listener. Again, everyone has something to be thankful for.

Life is what you focus on. Here, let me show you. Imagine you took your camera and went into the city and took pictures all day long. If you only focused on violence and took pictures of people fighting, then you and everyone else you showed the pictures to would picture the city being violent. If you only focused on people arguing, and captured that in the pictures, then you and everyone you showed the pictures to will see a city of frustration and one with high tension.

But, if focused your camera lens on something completely different and you captured pictures of people laughing and joking, then, you and everyone you showed the pictures to would see the city being happy and fun. If the pictures captured were of couples holding hands and kissing, then you and everyone else you showed them to would view the city as being a city of passion and love.

GRATITUDE has a way of illuminating the darkness of a bad situation. It is like having a flashlight in a dark castle full of treasures. If the flashlight is not on, you will only be lost in the darkness stumbling around in fear of what's around the corner. But once you turn the flashlight on, you will begin to discover treasures that were once hidden in the dark. When we begin to focus on what we *do* have, a sense of power and calm appreciation deep is created deep within.

Focus on being grateful for what you have instead of on what you do not have. Those who are grateful will be given more. If you focus on "lack" then you will bring more "lack" into your life, whether it is lack of money, time, friends, good health etc. Oprah Winfrey stated it very clearly, "The single greatest thing you can do to change your life today would be to start being grateful for what you have right now. And the more grateful you are, the more you get."

Remember, the Law of Attraction states that you bring to your life what you think about most. What you believe you deserve you will receive. The thoughts we send out have a certain vibrational frequency and will return with what it was sent out to retrieve.

If you are thinking lack you will bring lack. So, why not think abundance? What will it hurt? Would it be so bad to have an abundance of all the good things life has to offer?

It is healthy for you to want more and to do more in life. To want better grades, earn more money, or have the best relationship is natural. That is what keeps people motivated but remember if you are not grateful for where you are, who you are, and for what you have right now, then you will not be happy with more.

You can gain everything underneath the sun and you will still not be happy if you are not first happy with what you have and who you are in life right now.

I want you to understand something. I'm not talking about being grateful just to receive more. That is greed and being greedy will not only cause the Law of Reciprocation to stop, but it can and will also cause you to lose friends and the respect from your peers.

Rhonda Byrne puts it this way, "Be grateful for what you have now. As you begin to think about all the things in your life you are grateful for, you will be amazed at the never ending thoughts that come back to you of more things to be grateful for. You have to make a start, and then the law of attraction will receive those grateful thoughts and give you more just like them."

"When you are grateful, fear disappears and abundance appears"

Anthony Robbins

The news and media are full of the negativity around the world. They force feed you all the crimes, economic woes, terroristic news, and anything negative that is available from every corner of the globe. If this is all you see, then your view on life will be one of despair and hopelessness for all mankind.

If you choose to make a conscious effort and look around you, you will also see all the GOOD life has to offer. You will see acts of kindness everywhere. You will see the person helping the elderly across the street, someone anonymously paying for someone else's meal, or someone stopping on the side of the street to help a family with their flat tire.

You will see beauty in everything if you just take the time to become consciously aware. The brilliant colors the sun creates stretching across the sky as it sets in the evening, the laughter of a child, the relaxing walk around a lake with a loved one. Every day is a blessing.

Close your eyes and then open them. How do you see the world? This is your world. It is exactly how you want to see it. It is exactly what you think it is. If you think it is bad, then you will focus on bad situations to reinforce that belief and see a bad world. If you think it is good, then you will focus on positive situations to reinforce that belief, and see it as good.

Don't get me wrong. I'm not trying to suggest living in a fantasy world and you will never face negative life experiences. No one is immune to the difficulties of life.

What I am saying is that if you focus on the good and are grateful for what you do have and where you are in life, then you will begin to notice more to be grateful about, thus creating more positive experiences and situations to occur in your life.

Tough situations are only temporary. It can't rain forever. The sun has to come out and shine at some point. I want you to take a moment and think about the worst time in your life. It could have been a breakup, a death of someone close to you, losing your job, or being homeless. It was a bad time in your life, wasn't it? And yet, still, here you are.

Life goes on and it will continue to go on. You can look at all the things in life you have to be grateful for and enjoy each passing day, or you can simple be negative and let life pass you by.

Life will go on whether you are healthy or sick, wealthy or broke, grateful or not. But out of the options, how do you think life would be better lived? Would it be with a better level of health to enjoy each passing day with loved ones or being house-ridden and sick? Would life be better enjoyed with money to help others, pay your bills before they are due, and go on the vacations you want? Or would you rather be worried about how the bills will be paid?

Will life be better enjoyed wearing a smile from being joyful and happy on the inside from focusing on the blessings we have in our daily lives, or weighed down by wearing the coat of defeat by only focusing on the negative?

In life there are setback, losses, deaths, and disappointments. Life is not perfect. But without experiencing the negative, we can't truly appreciate the positive in life. If you have always been healthy your entire life and never once experienced sickness, you would not truly appreciate the level of health you have.

But, if you are extremely healthy and got sick with the flu and were confined to the bed for a few days, unable to live the life you were used to, then you would have a greater level of appreciation for your health.

"Gratitude is an attitude that hooks us up to our source of supply. And the more grateful you are, the closer you become to your maker, to the architect of the universe"

Bob Proctor

Let's pretend for a moment that today is your best friend's birthday, and you know that your best friend loves shoes more than anything else in this world. He or she has what would seem like a million pairs just sitting in their closet, all lined up by color and usage. Let's also pretend that the pair they wear more than any other pair, their most favorite pair, just got ruined by stepping in a dirty puddle of water.

If you had the option, knowing that your best friend's favorite pair of shoes was just ruined, to buy them a new pair just like the old pair, or giving them a gift card to the grocery store, what would you do? Would you give them something they love above all other things or something else? Hopefully you answered buying them the new pair of shoes.

Or, what if your girlfriend loves animals and her favorite animal is a turtle, and you were going to surprise her with a necklace. Would you surprise her with a necklace with a bicycle charm on it? No, of course not. It would be with a charm in the shape of a turtle. You will give her what she is passionate about. This is how the Universe, the Infinite Power is, with us. What we are grateful for and think about most often and believe we will receive, we will receive.

"Transformation begins with the renewing of your mind."

Romans 12:2

If you change your thoughts, then you can change your world. Once you begin to notice things you are grateful for, instead of what you don't like or are unhappy with at the present moment, you will begin to see more things you are grateful for. Things you may have been taking for granted and were not even aware of.

This is when a transformation will take place in your life. AWARENESS. Your mind will create new neurological receptors that will allow you to become more aware and appreciate the large and small things in life on a more consistent basis.

Changing your thoughts is like walking through a tall wheat field. The first pass through will be faint and not very visible. But the more passes you make through the same trail, the easier it will be seen and the less you have to search for it. Soon it will be so apparent that you will see it automatically without having to search for it.

This new awareness has the ability to singlehandedly change your life for the better. It has the potential to allow for the steady flow of abundance from the Universe to you. Like everything else in life, this is a skill that isn't necessarily given at birth. It is one that needs to be practiced. It has to be conditioned. Like learning closing techniques in sales or selecting the proper foods to eat for a balanced diet, it has to be practiced.

What I have found in my research is that those who are grateful for what they have enjoy life on a much deeper and more connected level. They are more connected with the Creator, with others, and with themselves. Their lives are more fulfilled and joyful. If you, like them, look for the small things in life to be grateful about, the big things will be even bigger.

"Faith without works is dead."

James 2:14-26

If you are unaware of what you have to be grateful for, then you be will unaware of the reasons to be happy. Happiness could be right in front of you and you wouldn't even know it. This is the reason new things have to be tried if you want Success and Happiness in your life. If the old way isn't working, then stop doing it. Look for a better way.

A new life requires a new way of thinking. Here are some simple, but POWERFUL exercises, to help you become aware of the things to be grateful for. These exercises will allow you to remove the dam that is blocking up your river of Abundance.

Ask Quality Questions.

(Remember dis-empowering questions get dis-empowering answers. Quality questions get quality answers.)

What am I grateful for in my relationship?

What am I grateful for in my health?

What am I grateful for in my job?

What am I grateful for in my career field?

What am I grateful for in my home?

What am I grateful for in my abilities?

What am I grateful for in my means of transportation?

What am I grateful for in my family?

What am I grateful for in my friends?

What am I grateful for in my spirituality?

Everyone has something to be grateful for. Write down these questions and their answers on a piece of paper. If at first you can only think of one answer, write it down. If you can think of 10, even better, write them down.

Keep a Gratitude Journal.

Grab a new journal, one that resonates with you. The sole purpose of this journal will be for writing about the things you are grateful for on a daily basis. It could be the phone call from a friend you haven't heard from in a while or a beautiful sunset. It could be the job promotion or a delicious dinner. It doesn't matter.

There are no right or wrong answers to write down, as long as you are grateful for them. Some days you will have more things to be grateful for than others, but try and write 7 things a day you are grateful for.

Here are a few of the benefits of keeping a Gratitude journal as reported from Happierhuman.com:

Benefits at a Glance

Results1	Study	Date
Keeping a gratitude journal caused participants to report 16% fewer physical symptoms, 19% more time spent exercising, 10% less physical pain, 8% more sleep, and 25% increased sleep quality.	Counting Blessings Versus Burdens	2003
The emotions of appreciation and gratitude shown to induce the relaxation response.	The Grateful Heart	2004
A gratitude visit reduced depressive symptoms by 35% for several weeks; a gratitude journal lowered depressive symptoms by 30%+ for as long as the practice was continued.	Positive Psychology Progress	2005
Patients with hypertension were instructed to count their blessings once a week. There was a significant decrease in their systolic blood pressure.	Gratitude: Effects on Perspectives and Blood Pressure	2007
Gratitude correlated with improved sleep quality ($r = .29$), less time required to fall asleep ($r = .20$), and increased sleep duration ($r = .14$).	Gratitude Influences Sleep Through the Mechanism of Pre-Sleep Cognitions	2009
Levels of gratitude significantly correlated with vitality and energy.	Multiple Studies	Many

"A five-minute-a-day gratitude journal can increase your long-term well-being by more than 10 percent. That's the same impact as doubling your income!" Amit Amin of happierhuman.com

Begin volunteering.

By giving to something greater than yourself, you will open up opportunities that will enable you to see what you have to be grateful for. Volunteering is not for you; it is for someone or something else. It is a selfless act, and also something that will fill one of our six human needs -- the need of contribution.

Write a short essay.

Write an essay about or to someone you are grateful for. It could be a friend, family member, teacher, student, significant other or someone who isn't even aware of what they have done. This will have a profound effect on you and your level of happiness and the one who receives the short essay.

Write a short essay.

Write an essay on a negative experience in your life and the positives you can find in that experience. Research shows it can change the meaning of the experience. Research also shows it can grant closure to the negative experience.

Start a Gratitude Jar

Grab a jar, a piece of paper, tape, and a marker. Write on the piece of paper "GRATITUDE" with the marker then tape it to the jar. Throughout the day when you notice something you are grateful for, write it down on a small piece of paper and put it in the jar.

At the end of each month, look back over what you have to be grateful for and at the end of the year, make it a tradition to look over your grateful experiences that took place over the past year.

Take a gratitude walk.

Take a nice relaxing walk around your neighborhood, your city, a lake or a park. Go somewhere that is peaceful and relaxing, to you, and begin to think of things or notice things you have to be grateful for. Smile and enjoy it.

Take the 7 Day Challenge.

Begin to unlock the floodgates of gratitude with this challenge. This 7-Day Challenge is one of the most powerful exercises you can involve yourself in.

Make a commitment to yourself that you will not complain, criticize or involve yourself in any kind negative talk for 7 days. And for 7 days you will commit to writing 7 things you are grateful for in your Gratitude Journal and smile for one minute 7 times a day. If you forget to write in your journal or realize that you have complained, criticized, or involved yourself in negative talk then you must start over. The same goes for smiling.

If gratitude is consistent and continuous then that which you are to be grateful for will be consistent and continuous.

If you go to work consistently at the same time every day and end at the same time everyday then your paycheck will be continuous. Stop going to work and you will stop getting paid. The only difference is one will pay you back what you believe you are worth, while the other will only pay you what someone feels your position is worth.

Be Thankful

"Be thankful that you don't already have everything you desire,

If you did, what would there be to look forward to?

Be thankful when you don't know something

For it gives you the opportunity to learn.

Be thankful for the difficult times

Gratitude

During those times you grow.

Be thankful for your limitations

Because they give you opportunities for improvement.

Be thankful for each new challenge

Because it will build your strength and character

Be thankful for your mistakes

They will teach you valuable lessons.

Be thankful when you're tired and weary

Because it means you've made a difference

It is easy to be thankful for the good things.

A life of rich fulfillment comes to those who are

Also thankful for the setbacks.

GRATITUDE can turn a negative into a positive.

Find a way to be thankful for your troubles

And they can become your blessings." - Author Unknown

Notes

You have just obtained the fourth Key: The Key of Gratitude. This Key will allow you to unlock the door of Abundance and see all that life has to be grateful for and allow more of it in your life.

Visualizing & Scripting

"Imagination is everything. It is the preview of life's coming attractions."

Albert Einstein

The book you are holding in your hands right now was once just an idea -- a thought. Those thoughts, ideas and all the research were then written down, spoken in speeches, and then compiled together and published. The clothes you are wearing were first created in someone's imagination. Someone had an idea of what they felt fashion was and created attire to match the images on the inside to be worn on the outside. Even the furniture you are sitting on started as an idea.

According to Merriam-Webster dictionary, "imagination" is *the act or power of forming a mental image of something not present to the senses or never before wholly perceived in reality*. These images and sensations that are created on the inside *can* and *will* manifest on the outside.

Everything begins in the mind's eye. Imagination is raw power in its simplest form. With your imagination, you begin to create the world in which you live in. You think, therefore, you create. It's that simple. The same is true for all things. The great thing that you are now learning is that you can also be a part of the creation instead of just taking part of the world around you.

"There are not limitations to the mind except those we acknowledge."

Napoleon Hill

Limitations

Visualizing and scripting can enhance all aspects of your life, from health, business, finances, relationships, and more. But before we discuss visualizing and scripting, I first want to talk to you about what holds you back from achieving the desired outcome you have in any given situation: limitations.

Limitations are ugly, desire-robbing LIARS. Limitations are the barriers which MUST be broken in order to achieve happiness and success. There are a number of "limitations," often referred to as excuses. Most people have and will offer up many excuses for the reason they are being held back from truly living the life they dream of.

Limitations can come in all shapes and sizes. I'm sure you can think of a few of them right now. It may be money "limitations" causing you to be unable to go on that dream vacation out of the country you have always wanted. It may be a physical "limitation" such as a lazy eye you feel that's holding you back from being the confident person you know you can be. It could be knowledge "limitation" that is keeping you from the particular school you want to attend or holding you back from starting your own business. Who knows? There are thousands of excuses or "limitations" people feel are keeping them from living their dreams.

Do you know what a limitation really is? Think about it. A limitation only has perceived boundaries and a perceived ceiling. Limitations cause you to become nervous, fearful, and imprison you to your comfort zone. And we can't grow in the comfort zone.

It's like being the new kid in class and the others kids heard you were fast. So now they want you to race against the fastest kid in their class. At first, you get a little nervous because you look at the other kid and notice he is much taller than you. In fact, he is the tallest kid in the entire class. He just looks fast standing there. Even the shoes on his feet look fast.

You begin to think of reasons why you shouldn't race him, such as; *if you get beat you will be embarrassed, what if you trip and fall in front of everyone, and what if you run differently than the other kids and they make fun of you?* You begin to think of excuses.

But you decide to reject the negative thoughts that are running through your mind and face him anyway. You stand next to him at the starting line on the playground. You look up at him and flash a smile of confidence. Both of you get in your starting positions and the countdown begins. 3, 2, 1, GO!

You take off like a bolt of lightning. Your little legs pump with all your might and before you know it you are at the finish line......waiting for your competition.

Have you figured out what a limitation is? A limitation is only a CHALLENGE. That is it, simply a challenge and nothing more. Limitations are not a death sentence to your goal, unless you decide they are. A challenge can be faced and conquered!

From this moment forward, I no longer want you to call them limitations. I want you to refer to them as challenges, because that is all they are: challenges. When you are faced with a challenge, you have two options. You can either cower in fear and let life and everything in it walk all over you like a doormat, or you can choose to stand firm, plant your feet and meet the challenge head on. Do what needs to be done and conquer it! This is your life! Conquer it! Desire it! Live it!

"Do just once what others say you couldn't do and you will never pay attention to their limitations again."

James Cook

The quickest, easiest and BEST way to conquer your challenges begins in your mind. Napoleon Hill, one of the greatest writers of success said it perfectly, "Whatever the mind can conceive and believe, it can achieve." The victory must first take place in the mind. Now, I'm not only talking about the victories held in the sports world, but victories in all areas of your life.

If being overweight is your challenge, then conquer it. If money is your challenge, then conquer it. If the relationship you are in is not where it can be, then conquer it. If you feel stuck or feel as if you just don't have enough time to get all the things done that need to get done, then conquer it. Whatever your challenge is in life right now, CONQUER IT!

The victory and the manifestation of your internal desires first begins in the mind. Remember that this book you are reading, the clothes you are wearing, and the furniture you are sitting on right now were all first visually created in the mind. Visualize and have faith and believe. Not having belief in your desires is like having a car with no gas. It may be great to look at and talk about, but it will never get you anywhere.

It's sad to see so many people live their lives in a dull and unenthusiastic manner. They go through their days lifeless because of self-imposed limitations. Self-imposed limitations are thoughts or beliefs that will only limit your ability to live your life to the fullest.

At times it may even be knowledge of something that has set the limitation in life. The knowledge can be true or false. For instance, if you had dreams and aspirations to go to the NBA and you were only 5'7" and you had "knowledge" that the average height of NBA players is roughly 6' 7'," then this "knowledge" could create self-imposed limitations. It would say that you physically would not make it to the NBA due to your height and may not be able to dunk a basketball due to the fact there is so much distance between you and the rim.

Anthony Jerome "Spud" Webb didn't let the knowledge of what was possible and impossible keep him from becoming the shortest man to play in the NBA at the time, and didn't keep him from winning the Slam Dunk contest in 1986. True, Spud Webb was short in comparison to the other players, but he was not limited. Too many people will let self-imposed limitations create the boundaries of their lives. They let them dictate what they can and cannot do. And if you do not get rid of them, they can rob you of your dreams.

Knowledge says that due to the sheer weight and shape of the bumble bee, it cannot fly. Well, guess what? Someone forgot to tell the bumble bee this "knowledge" because the species is able to fly. Not once has the bumble bee been trapped and held down by weight and shape of his physical limitations.

"Self-imposed limitations are shackles that hold us down and prevent us from achieving our potential."

Rob MacDonald

Self-imposed limitations are self-inflicted limitations such as; *I'm not smart enough, I'm not tall enough, I'm not strong enough, I'm not confident enough, I'm not pretty or good looking enough, I'm afraid of failing, I don't deserve it.* They are created by you. Self-imposed limitations will only keep you from achieving your life's goals. If you fall into the trap of limitations, rest assured your realm of possibilities will shrink tremendously in size. Limitations will keep you grounded and stuck while others like the bumble bee and Spud Webb fly and do the impossible.

The Secret to:

Overcoming Self-Imposed Limitations.
A simple 3-step process:

First. Determine what your self-imposed limitations are. If you are unaware of what needs to be changed, then how can you change it?

Does your self-defeating limitation say that you are: *too fat, too skinny, too old, too young, too smart, too dumb, too broke, too wealthy, too depressed, too introverted, too ugly?* What are your imposed limitations? What "excuse" do you use when you need to take action?

Second. Doubt the current limitation. Understand that a limitation is something YOU believe. A belief doesn't have to be true to be believed. A belief is only a thought that has been reinforced through experiences, personal opinions or opinions of others, as well as things seen or read about.

So, doubt the limiting belief. By doubting the limiting belief, you are taking a sledgehammer and breaking the foundation of it. By breaking the foundation, you are able to take it up, throw it away, and replace it with something that will empower you. So let's doubt the belief, to break the foundation, by asking questions.

9 Powerful questions to begin to change your disempowering beliefs

1. Where did this belief come from?

2. How is this belief affecting me and my life negatively?

3. If I don't change this limiting belief, how will it affect me spirituality?

4. If I don't change this limiting belief, how will it affect my finances?

5. If I don't change this limiting belief, how will it affect my family?

6. If I don't change this limiting belief, how will it affect my mental health?

7. If I don't change this limiting belief, how will it affect my physical health?

8. What would I do if I didn't have this belief?

9. How would my life be better if I didn't have this belief?

Third. Replace the limiting belief. Replace the belief that is holding you back with one that empowers you. And reinforce it. By removing the perceived limitation, your realm of opportunities opens up and becomes endless. The reinforcement will cause actions to match your belief.

You must remember the old belief has to be replaced with a new one. If not, the old limiting belief will only resurface.

If the limiting belief was, "I'm not smart enough," then the new belief could be, "I am very intelligent and have the ability and resources to educate myself on whatever I wish." And reinforce it by recalling times when you learned something new. Recall times when someone complimented you on being smart and doing well. Reinforcement of a thought causes a thought to become a belief.

If it is the limiting belief of, "I'm not pretty enough or good looking enough," then the new belief could be, "I am very attractive." And then reinforce it with times you felt attractive, times when someone told you that you were pretty, or times when you caught someone of the opposite sex checking you out.

The only person keeping you from breaking through your limitations or "challenges" and realizing your true potential is you. Get out of your own way! Be the person you were meant to be! Achieve the goals you were meant to achieve! Live the life you were meant to live!

"Dare to visualize a world in which your most treasured dreams have become true."

Ralph Marston - Greatday.com

Visualize

The mind is constantly working to create the reality that it is shown. It is your God-given right to discover and use this inner power of thought and emotions. Use the power that you have hidden inside of you that can and will unlock the doors of abundance in your life. Even though you cannot see it, its power and your power is stronger than you can imagine. Once this knowledge is achieved and applied, the world is at your fingertips.

Your mind is your personal servant and works to make sure your life is consistent with the internal dialogue and images created. If you are constantly thinking and visualizing thoughts of abundance, then the mind will manifest abundance in your life. If you constantly think and visualize negative thoughts, then you will experience negativity in your life.

The reason for this is that if your mind doesn't create and manifest what it is shown, and you experience situations that contradict these images that you believe to be true, then you will think that you are crazy. And your mind will not let this happen.

Look at it like this. Your mind is a genie with a huge ego. It is strong, powerful, and is always right. Your mind will say, "I'm not going to let anything happen to contradict what I believe to be true. I am perfect. If you are showing me that you live an opulent and affluent life, then I must create it. If you are showing me that you are lazy, then I create that too. Your wish is my command."

So, it creates what it is shown and believed to be true in your heart of hearts. For instance, have you ever had a job interview or were going to meet the parents of someone you were dating and you felt confident and just knew that everything was going to go smooth, perfect, and effortlessly? And it did! You got the job or the parents loved and adored you. Well, this is visualizing in action. What you visualize and know to be true will be true.

So, be careful what you tell your mind to create. Because your mind will not discern right from wrong or good from bad and then select what would be the best option for you. It will only create what you tell it to create.

"Create the highest grandest vision possible for your life, because you become what you believe."

Oprah Winfrey

The technique of visualization is simple and can be very fun. It is like being a child. You can imagine anything you want and no one can stop you. No one can limit your imagination. But remember to watch your thoughts because they will become your world. Once you begin visualizing and start to see the internal thoughts manifest into external experiences, the more your confidence will grow, and the easier it will be for you. Think about it. I'm sure the first time you drove a car was pretty nerve racking.

First, you nervously get in and adjust the seat and mirrors, hoping they are in the perfect position because you will need them shortly. You grab the key and slide it into the ignition, and slowly turn it until you hear the car start up, which stirs up excitement and anxiousness inside of your stomach. Soon, you will be driving down the road heading to your destination with other cars whizzing by you, and there will be turns to take and stops to make along the way. You put it into gear and slowly press the gas, looking in all directions just to make sure there are no other vehicles that can interfere with you. And this is all before you get out of the driveway.

But the more you drove, the more your confidence grew and the easier it became for you. Before you knew it, you were in autopilot and driving without having to consciously think about it.

Visualization is the same way. You can visualize your way to your perfect life. You can dream of how great things will be, except you will now do it in present tense. And before you know it, like driving a car, you will be in autopilot living the life that was once just a thought.

A visualization exercise you can implement into your life is *The Shower of Emotional Cleansing.* This exercise will help you to rid yourself of negative feelings and emotions you have inside of you quickly and easily. Remember, no one's life is perfect. Every single one of us has had negative life experiences happen to us, some more than others and some worse than others. Either way, they happen to all of us, and no one can hide from them.

When these negative experiences occur, often times pieces of them stay with us and are hard to get rid of, because they are hard to forgive. Bitterness towards those experiences usually causes inner turmoil. From this inner turmoil, more negative thoughts and ideas are created, and if we are not careful, they will manifest in our lives. Luckily, we have the power inside of us to change it. We have the POWER to rid ourselves of this negativity. We can choose to take The Shower of Emotional Cleansing. This exercise is one I have taught others and one that I myself use, to get the "gunk" out. It's a quick and easy way to clear your mind of negative life experiences and feelings and start fresh.

This is a very easy exercise. First, I want you to visualize getting into the shower and turning the water to your favorite temperature. Now relax and feel the water pouring over you from your head down to your feet. The more the water pours over you, the more relaxed you feel.

Now think about all the things that are bothering you. Think about all the bad things that have happened to you. Think about all the hurt you have experienced or caused. Think about any physical, mental, financial, or spiritual "limitations" you feel you may have. Think of any negative emotions you have. When you think about them, picture them forming above your head, like a cartoon bubble.

Now visualize that the water that is pouring out of the showerhead is pouring out over each and every one of the "bubbles of negativity." Picture the water penetrating them and distorting the pictures that were created inside of them.

What was once easily seen as negative images and emotional distress should now only be bubbles of contorted, unclear images.

Now visualize the cartoon bubbles slowly filling up with water. They are filling all the way up. The weight of the water is now causing the bubbles to grow heavier and heavier until they begin to drop to the bottom of the shower like large rain drops. You see the bubbles hit the bottom of the shower and begin washing down the drain one by one, never to be seen or heard from again.

Now recall positive emotions and experiences that you have had in your life. Times you achieved, times you felt loved, times you felt happy, times you felt joy and peace. Think about them vividly. Really feel the excitement and the love and the happiness. Really feel the joy and peace. Let these feelings consume your mind and body. Once you do this, all that will remain are the powerful positive memories and emotions. These memories are what will create more happiness and success in your life.

If at any time a memory that has been washed down the drain tries to resurface, remind yourself that it has all been washed away, and if you need to, visualize yourself turning the hot water on, scalding the unwanted power-robbing memory down the drain one last time, and this time for good.

Everything in life is a choice. You choose to do something or you choose not to do something; there is no trying. To prove this to you, I want you to try holding your breath, right now. Ok, what happened? Did you hold it, did you continue breathing or did you try to hold your breath? Either you held it or you didn't, there was no trying.

Once you choose to take the Shower of Emotional Cleansing, you should be feeling lighter and freer. Choices are what determine the paths we will take in life. If you make the right choices today, you will have a right tomorrow. If you make the wrong choices today, then you will have a wrong tomorrow. Your choice.

You are able to choose your thoughts, which will in return determine your mood, which directly affects the actions you take. So, be careful what you think. Some say watch your words, I say watch your thoughts. Your thoughts are the seeds planted in the subconscious garden of your mind from where your life is grown.

We have all heard, "Words have Power." This is powerfully true. But where do words come from? They are cultivated in our thoughts. That's right, in the garden of your mind! You have to clear the garden of your mind of the negative weeds and plant positive seeds.

"Whatever we plant in our subconscious mind and nourish with repetition and emotion will one day become reality."

Earl Nightingale

This is a technique I call, *The Garden*. I use it to clear my mind of the negative weeds and plant positive seeds. You will first begin this technique by relaxing the mind and body by meditation. If you are unfamiliar with meditation, I would strongly suggest looking it up online and doing some research on it. Research has shown meditation to increase test scores, lower blood pressure, and increase the ability to focus, along with numerous other positive benefits. Meditation is also a powerful tool which will greatly assist you with manifesting.

While in the meditative state, I picture a garden. Now, this is no small garden. It is a large 100 square yard garden, covered with weeds from one end to the other. I then picture a new bright green tractor coming over and tilling up the entire garden. While this tractor is tilling up the old unwanted soil, it is also chopping up all the negative unwanted weeds into the smallest of particles.

When the first tractor's job is finished, I then have another tractor that comes and pushes all of the dirt away. As he sweeps back and forth, he leaves no trace of the old soil or weeds that were previously occupying the land. The only thing left is a large empty hole with nothing but potential just waiting for me to do something with it. Then I smile, because I know that everything negative that was once planted there has been uprooted, and the garden is ready for the new nutrient rich soil to be laid. Dump trucks dump load after load, filling up the once empty lot with the best and finest soil needed for growing.

After the soil is deposited from the dump trucks and leveled out, I begin to optimistically plant in my new garden all the desires I wish to have. I plant everything from the perfect relationship that is full of trust, communication, and fun to the career that I could not be happier with that provides me with more than enough money, fulfillment, and joy.

I also plant the seeds of the best health anyone could ask for mentally and physically and seeds of adventure and travel. The seeds of happiness and success are seen throughout the garden. I deserve only the best, and nothing but the best will be planted in the garden of my life. You too, deserve nothing but the best. God wants you to have nothing but the best.

What seeds would you like to plant? Because this is the best part; you get to choose what it is you want to plant in your garden and what will manifest in your life. Plant your seeds, and you must nourish and cultivate your garden with only positive thoughts and images.

Nourish it through reading and learning about what it is you want to have. If it is money, then read and learn about stocks, real estate, investments, savings, or starting your own business. Then picture having it. Picture it in full color and detail and flood this image with emotions. Live in the moment. Feel as if you already have it and are living the life.

If it is the perfect relationship, then picture you and your significant other doing everything you want to do together. And again, picture it with full detail and engulfed in positive emotions. If you enjoy a day on the beach, then picture you and your companion enjoying a day on the white sand beach of your favorite vacation getaway. Feel the cool breeze mixed with the warm sun on your skin as the two of you take a stroll feeling the sand beneath your toes and the water rushing up against your ankles as the tide rolls in. Feel the touch of their fingers intertwined in yours.

Maybe it's going out to a nice dinner, or maybe it's traveling and exploring another country. It doesn't matter what the scenario is. All you have to do is play it out in the theater of your mind exactly how it looks and feels. You want to see it. You want to feel it. Picture the two of you with perfect communication skills and with the feeling of complete trust. Feel the strong unbreakable frequency of love resonating between the two of you. Engulf yourself in the feelings and emotions.

Whatever it is you desire to manifest into your life, use the powerful technique of visualization. Athletes are taught the power of visualization and use it often to improve their skill level.

In the article, *Teaching Athletes Visualization and Mental Imagery Skills*, written by Dr. David Yukelson Ph.D. of Penn State University, he says, "Many athletes use imagery as a mental training skill to build confidence and a feeling of readiness prior to competition. It can also be used as a cognitive technique to plan competition strategies, rehearse game plans, affirm what you want to occur, or as a coping skill strategy to stay calm and composed under pressure.

Everyone possesses the ability to use imagery, like anything else, it is a skill that must be developed and practiced."

In the same article, Dr. Yukelson explains the crucial element that most people are missing for the power of visualization to work. Dr. Yukelson says, "The key is to program your mind, muscles, and emotions for success, and to make your imagery as vivid, realistic, and detailed as possible. When you vividly imagine yourself getting ready for competition, your central nervous system becomes programmed for success. With authentic practice and specific application it's as if the activity you visualized has already happened!"

According to Nicole Detling, a sports psychologist with the United States Olympic team, "The more an athlete can image the entire package, the better it's going to be." This is true for all of us, not just athletes. The more vividly we create the image in the theater of our mind, the more we are programming ourselves for what it is we want! The more we visualize the entire picture, the better it's going to be. We can use this simple technique for ALL areas of our lives; happiness, success, financial freedom, perfect relationships, the job promotion, ANYTHING!

There was a case study where two businessmen had a product to sell: luxury mattresses. The first fellow decided to approach as many retailers as he could to get his mattress in their stores. Through a lot of struggle and hard work, he eventually got a few contracts. But the money did not flood into his account very quickly, and he was easily discouraged. Unfortunately for this first businessman, he never reached

*his goal of making $500,000 because he soon gave up on his
tiring venture.*

*The second fellow did something very different. He spent a
few days thinking about how he would sell his mattresses.
While the first guy was out pounding the pavement, this
second businessman spent his days lounging around in his
garden, thinking of innovative ways to sell his mattresses. He
ended up creating an interesting marketing system that
landed him big accounts with various hotels. Consequently,
the money started flooding into his bank account very
quickly and furiously. He was happy indeed. He met his goal
of making $500,000 profit and in fact, exceeded it!
(Article form UpstartSuccess.com)*

Visualize whatever it is you desire in perfect detail. Get all of
your senses involved. The more involved all your senses are,
the better. You want your emotions to be fully engaged. The
stronger the emotions and the clearer the visualization is,
the better. Remember, your mind only knows what you tell
it to be true and will act accordingly. Begin sowing the seeds
of happiness, fun, greatness, peace, love and prosperity,
now. Accept them fully in your mind, NOW!

Picture the perfect life playing out as if you are already living
it. Picture yourself heading home from a great day at work
at the job you truly love. See yourself driving your dream car
along the winding roads until you reach your driveway.
Picture yourself slowly pulling up the driveway that is

beautifully landscaped along each side as if it were in a magazine.

You park in the first bay of your 3-car garage. See yourself happily walking over and opening the front door of your new home, and then hearing the sound of the door closing behind. See your perfect companion greeting you with a smile and an embracing hug that just resonates love through and through. Feel the smile on your face as you gaze out of the floor to ceiling windows to the back of the house and catch the sun setting. Feel all the joy and love of living in the home you always dreamed of with the one you always dreamed of.

Scripting

Have you heard the commonly used phrase, "the pen is mightier than the sword?" If so, have you ever stopped and wondered why people use this expression? I want you to think about it for a moment. How could something so small and dull in comparison to a sword be considered mightier?

Could a sword, an instrument of death that is several feet in length and can be wielded with precision and accuracy and strike fear into the eyes and hearts of men, really be considered inferior to an instrument only a few inches in length and used to create words, thoughts, and ideas? The answer is YES. Why?

The pen is more powerful and far more superior to the sword due to the simple fact that there is unlimited energy and power in writing. It's not the pen itself but what the pen is capable of that transcends the sword.

With the pen, you can write not only about your past, your thoughts, and your emotions but also about your ideas, your dreams, and YOUR FUTURE. With the pen, you can write the book of YOUR life.

The pen has been the reason countless couples have fallen in love. I'm sure you can think of a love poem or love letter you yourself have either written or read right now. And what instrument created those works of art? That's right. The Pen! The pen is the reason countries at war have come together in their time of need and a treaty was signed to bring peace. The pen is the reason mergers have brought financial abundance to those involved.

The pen is the reason YOU can fall in love with your life and be fulfilled. The pen can bring peace to YOU and those around you. The pen can bring YOU financial abundance.

The pen and your imagination will enable you to write the life YOU wish to have, not the life others want you to have. Sometimes parents and family members or even friends and peers can offer up suggestions of how your life should be lived. They do not mean any harm by the suggestions they are spilling on you.

I refer to them as suggestions because no matter who the person is or how aggressively they are "suggesting" something to you, it is ultimately your decision what you do with your life.

"Our lives are a sum total of the Choices we have made."

Dr. Wayne Dyer

No one can force you to do something you do not want to do. You have a choice. All anyone can do is suggest you do something. Suggestions can include the type of relationships you should have or even who you should date. They might suggest a particular career you would be "perfect" for or the type of car you should purchase because "it received great reviews." They might suggest you change certain habits you have or create other habits you don't have.

All they are doing is simply suggesting things they either wish they had, have done or would do, if they had it to do all over again. This is your life. CREATE IT. LIVE IT, not theirs.

A friend might suggest a sales job for you because of your ability to build rapport so easily and quickly, but you may not have the slightest interest in sales. Your passions may be the complete opposite. You ideal career field may be in psychology, not sales. You might find fulfillment and joy in learning about the human mind and helping others.

If their suggestions do not resonate with you, then simply let them go. Do not entertain the suggestions in your mind;

instead relax and enjoy the beauty of your imagination and perform the creative exercise of Scripting.

You get to write about the relationships, the fun, the vacations, the financial abundance, the growth and contribution. And all this is resting in one of the most powerful instruments man has ever had the privilege to hold in his hand: the pen. Use the power of the pen often. It is also important to smile and be happy when you do it. Put yourself in the moment you are writing about using all of the body's senses you can.

Scripting is the external form of ideas and dreams from the endless internal realm of possibilities. Remember, the internal realm of possibilities is far greater than the external factors. This is the reason Albert Einstein said, "Imagination is more important than knowledge. For knowledge is limited to all we now know and understand, while imagination embraces the entire world, and all there ever will be to know and understand."

Dr. Joyce Rennolds, who I view as the foremost expert in scripting today, holds a scripting class in Atlanta, GA. This class is where I learned an abundance of information on and about the power of scripting.

Dr. Rennolds explained that to begin scripting, you must first "find a journal that feels good, looks good, resonates with you and has high vibrations." You should also dedicate, date and sign the inside cover or the first page of the journal. She goes on to say, "Your journal will house your inner most thoughts and desires. It will be the basis of understanding that the Power of The Infinite Mind of God is within you and that you can script out your future just the way you want it! With the process of scripting you are building an energy field, activating the law of attraction, putting out for what you want, therefore it is wise if you script every day."

"History will be kind to me for I intend to write it."

Winston Churchill

Be detailed in your visualizing and writing, or scripting as it is referred to. The more detail and emotion you put in, the stronger it will become and the more quickly it can manifest. You are the creator of your reality. Script it and visualize it in detail and with great emotion and get ready for the creation to begin.

Reality is relative. The reality you create and live is YOUR perception of reality. As discussed in previous chapters, the title or label you give a situation is that and only that because you titled or labeled that particular instance that. A bad situation is only bad because you labeled it bad. A circumstance is great because you labeled it great.

Your mind is a gift from God. And this gift that you have been blessed with is overflowing with the Infinite Power of God, which includes the power to change, the power to influence, the power to prosper, the power to create happiness, and more. They are all there for you to control if you understand how. Anything you desire to have is readily available to you once you understand the Formula and make the choice to believe it to be true.

You have to remember that the secret is to get your emotions involved. The mind only knows what you are telling it. It does not know the difference between past and future, or false images from reality. It only knows what you tell it and how you feel about what you are telling it, and it works to create that as your REALITY. Your life will be what you feel, and what you show yourself on the movie of your mind.

If the energy is not there, then leave. The beauty of each morning is that it is a new beginning. Today is a new day. One in which you were blessed with the freedom of choice. That freedom of choice is power. You have the power! You have the power to change the situations and circumstances in your life. Script and Visualize the life you desire as if you already have it and you will bring power of the universe with you. The Power of God is inside of you and wanting to create.

You get to choose if things stay the same or if they change. You get to choose if you feel good about yourself and make the most of every possible situation or if you sit on your pity pot and whine about everything. Your choice.

I want you to know you are blessed beyond measure. You have been blessed with more power than you realize. You are a child of God and made in his image. You have the power to create the life you want. It is your choice.

Notes

You have just discovered the fifth and final Key:
The Key of Visualization. Use this Key to see things
as you want them to be, not as they are.

Conclusion

Congratulations! You have just finished reading the simplest self-help book ever written. The 5 simple Keys you just discovered can unlock the door of unlimited possibilities and abundance in your life. It can grant you the happiness and success you have been searching for.

The Universe and all its amazing power are there and WAITING to create on your behalf. The better the understanding you have of the 5 Key Principles the better you will be equipped to create the life you want with ease. I would recommend you re-reading this book several times and taking notes until you feel and believe the 5 Simple Keys are a part of you.

An architect does not design one home or one building and become a master designer. He has to condition his skills to become a master designer. Once you condition your skills with the 5 Principles then you, like the architect, will become a master designer. But, you will not be designing houses or buildings. You, my dear friend, will be the master designer of YOUR LIFE!

Get excited and get ready to experience your newly empowered journey today.....

Use the Key of Law of Attraction to attract to your life what you think about most and truly believe. Ask, Believe, and Receive.

Use the Key of Forgiveness to unlock yourself from your past. The past is gone and has no control over you. Forgive and become free.

Use the Key of Positive Self-Image to be who YOU want to be. Be confident, be happy, be successful. You will reach as high as YOU think you can.

Use the Key of Gratitude to unlock the river of abundance to flow over you. The more you are grateful for the more you will be given to be grateful for. Gratitude is Paramount.

Use the Key of Visualizing to see things as you want them to be, not as they are. Visualize, as Albert Einstein called it, "Life's coming attractions."

Conclusion

Your new life, the life you truly desire, is only 5 simple Keys away. This is your life and you deserve to enjoy it. You deserve to be happy. You deserve to be successful.

Live the life that others what to live. Live the life that others ask; Why are you are always happy? Why does everything always seem to go your way? What is your secret? What do you know that everyone else doesn't?

When others ask you these questions all you have to do is smile and tell them, "It's simple. The life you desire, like mine, is only 5 Simple Keys away" and hand them a copy of this book

Quotes & Affirmations

I firmly believe in reading something positive every day. Something you see, read, or hear could possibly change the course of your day or even your life.

Looking at positive quotes, affirmations, movies, or listening to songs, and positive people on a daily basis will begin to build a warehouse of positive thoughts inside your mind. This warehouse will soon become part of the subconscious mind and work for your better good without you even trying.

According to Dr. Loretta J. Standley, "It takes 40 days to impress upon the unconscious "reacting" mind all that you desire and dream. Then it becomes automatic behavior in the conscious "acting" mind. Affirmations are the same as doing any type of repetitive exercise to change or learn a new behavior." She suggests writing or repeating affirmations that you want to be a part of you 40 times daily for 40 days.

Quotes

"We cannot solve our problems with the same thinking that created them" - Albert Einstein

"You can live your life angry, bitter, mad at somebody or even guilty, not letting go of your own mistakes, but you won't receive the good things God has in store for you." - Joel Osteen

"When you are grateful fear disappears and abundance appears." - Anthony Robbins

"The vast majority of people are born, grow up, struggle, and go through life in misery and failure, not realizing that it would be just as easy to switch over and get exactly what they want out of life, not recognizing that the mind attracts the thing it dwells upon." - Napoleon Hill

"Imagination is everything. It is the preview of life's coming attractions." - Albert Einstein

"All that we are is a result of what we have thought." - Buddha

"We are shaped by our thoughts, we become what we think. When the mind is pure, joy follows like a show that never leaves." - Buddha

"Greater self-esteem produces greater success, and greater success produces more high self-esteem, so it keeps spiraling up." - Jack Canfield

"A man is but a product of his thoughts. What he thinks he becomes." – Gandhi

"Whatever your mind can conceive and believe it can achieve." - Napoleon Hill

"For as he thinks in his heart, so is he." - Proverbs 23:7

"I can do all things through Christ who strengthens me." - Philippians 4:13

"For God did not give us a spirit of fear, but of power, of love, and of a sound mind." - 2 Timothy 1:7

"When you change the way you look at things, the things you look at will change." - Dr. Wayne Dyer

"You create your own Universe as you go along."
- Winston Churchill

"Leave your excuses behind, and you will begin to attract wealth." - Joe Vitale

"We are what we pretend to be, so be careful what you pretend to be." - Kurt Vonnegut

"Let a person radically alter his thought and he will be astonished at the rapid transformation in the material conditions of his life." - James Allen

"What this power is I cannot say. All I know is that it exists."
- Alexander Graham Bell

"Nurture your mind with great thoughts, for you will never go any higher than you think." - Benjamin Disraeli

"By choosing your thoughts, and by selecting which emotional currents you will release and which you will reinforce, you determine the quality of your Light. You

determine the effects you will have on others and the nature of the experience of your life." - Gary Zukav

"It is impossible for you to be angry and laugh at the same time. Anger and laughter are mutually exclusive and you have the power to choose either." - Dr. Wayne Dyer

"And the Lord said, if you had faith as a grain of mustard seed, you might say to this sycamore tree, Be you plucked up by the root, and be you planted in the sea; and it should obey you." - Luke 17:6

"You can't heal what you don't acknowledge." - Jack Canfield

"It is in your moments of decision that your destiny is shaped." - Anthony Robbins

"Forgiveness is about empowering yourself, rather than empowering your past." - T.D. Jakes

"Conflict cannot survive without your participation."
- Dr. Wayne Dyer

"Love is the ability and willingness to allow those that you care for to be what they choose for themselves without any insistence that they satisfy you." - Dr. Wayne Dyer

"Your purpose explains what you are doing with your life. Your vision explains how you are living your purpose. Your goals enable you to realize your vision." - Bob Proctor

"Thoughts become things. If you see it in your mind, you will hold it in your hand." - Bob Proctor

"You can have, do or be anything you want." – Joe Vitale

"There are laws of the universe and if you practice them they will respond to you" - Michael Beckwith

"There's enough for everyone. If you believe it, if you can see it, if you act from it, it will show up for you. That's the truth" - Michael Beckwith

"Overcome your barriers, intend the best, and be patient. You will enjoy more balance, more growth, more income, and more fun!" - Jack Canfield

"You always get what you unconsciously believe and expect." - Joe Vitale

"Whether you think you can or think you can't, you are right." - Henry Ford

Affirmations:

Health

I look young and I feel young.

My body is functioning at peak performance, mentally and physically.

My body becomes healthier and stronger with every breath I take.

Every day in every way I am getting healthier and healthier.

I only think positive thoughts and in return I receive a healthy mind and body.

Happiness is a choice and I choose to be happy.

I wake up each day with strength in my heart, health in my body, and clarity in my mind.

I always have fun and always enjoy myself.

I have an abundance of energy every day and sleep great every night.

I fall asleep quickly and effortlessly.

I have power over all habits in my life. I have the power to easily create new habits to better my life or break bad habits that are hindering it.

I look good and feel good inside and out.

I am open to receiving all the healing energies of the Universe.

I maintain optimum health daily with ease.

I appreciate my healthy mind and body.

My healthy thoughts are constantly creating my healthy mind and body.

My pure thoughts create a pure and powerful mind.

Prosperity

I easily earn $1,000,000 a year.

God blesses me with his unlimited resources

I can achieve anything I set my mind to.

I attract the right people to me.

I am financially free.

I do what I want when I want as money flows to me often.

Large sums of money come easily, effortlessly, and often to me.

I find the good in all things and because of this good things come to me with abundance.

I only attract good things to me and my life and those around me.

I possess the qualities needed to be extremely successful

Creative energy surges through me and leads me to new and brilliant ideas.

I succeed in all that I do

Unlimited possibilities present themselves to me which assist me in reaching the next level of success.

I can achieve anything I set my mind to.

I am attracting money now.

I always have more than enough money to pay bills, save, and to have fun with.

I am prosperous, healthy, and happy.

Abundance in all things good is mine.

Life is easy.

I give generously and it causes happiness for others and myself.

I love money and money loves me.

I attract money and money is attracted to me.

I am debt free as money flows to me easily and often.

The things I enjoy doing passionately bring large sums of money to me.

Relationships

Many people look up to me and recognize my worth; I am admired.

I love everyone and everything and everyone and everything loves me

Divine order is over my life and all of its situations.

Every situation always works out for my benefit.

I attract the right people into my life.

I have a strong, happy, and faithful relationship. One that is full of fun and excitement.

I love who I am.

People love to talk to me and be around me.

My relationship gets stronger and better with each passing day.

Love, trust, and happiness dwell in the midst of me and my relationship.

I only attract relationships to my life.

The past of my relationship is healed and it is not stronger and more trusting than ever.

I deeply respect and cherish my partner as they do me.

I am overflowing with gratitude for my happy relationship

My relationship is naturally healthy and happy

With each passing day I am grow happier and happier in my relationship

I communicate honestly and lovingly

Romance improves my relationship

Sales

I am very persuasive.

I close every deal with ease.

I am the top producer in the company.

Deals come to me with ease and are happy with the service I provide.

Referrals come to me often.

I am a professional and I carry myself professionally.

Clients love to pay me good money to help them better their lives.

I make new sales every day.

My clients are happy and easy to deal with.

My commissions are getting larger and larger with each paycheck I receive.

I earn great money doing what I love.

I know my product better than anyone else.

I am the best at what I do.

I build rapport quickly and easily and put people at ease.

People feel comfortable and at ease when dealing with me.

I am an effective and powerful presenter and sales person.

I am charismatic and attract high end clients with ease.

I easily and consistently improve myself personally and professionally.

I focus on today's greatest opportunities and they always come to fruition.

Other

I have complete faith and belief in God and in my abilities I was blessed with.

I visualize for ten minutes every day.

I am passionate about everything I do.

I am greatness.

Love and joy radiate from me and draw to me the same in return.

I am beautiful.

I am fun.

I am confident in all that all I do. I am confident in the way that I walk, in the way that I talk, and in the way I carry myself.

Today is rich with opportunities and I open my heart to receive them.

Today I receive my prosperity from both expected and unexpected sources.

It is my natural birthright to be happy and successful.

I am becoming more successful with each passing day.

My life overflows with endless opportunities and prosperity.

I am happy, successful and fulfilled.

I am guided in my every step by Spirit who leads me towards what I must know and do.

I am blessed. And, I am thankful for my blessings.

I love speaking in front of crowds.

People come from all over to hear me speak.

I speak slow, plain and clear. I speak smooth and articulate my words.

The Infinite Mind of God works through me and for me in every way.

I am grateful for my life and I live it with passion.

I find the good in all things and because of this good things come to me with abundance.

Love and joy radiate from me and draw to me the same in return.

Say or write these daily to see results that will amaze and delight you. Feel free to email me any stories you have of how your life has changed for the better from the information and exercises discussed within this book. I would love to hear from you.

May you be blessed with happiness and success in all you do.

Contact me:

lifecoachdannycole@gmail.com

Or visit my webpage

theformulacoach.com

theformulacoachingsystems.com